REACHING LIGHT

REACHING LIGHT

EDITED BY DEVIN JOHNSTON

/

SELECTED POEMS

FLOOD EDITIONS, CHICAGO

/

ROBERT ADAMSON

Published by Flood Editions
www.floodeditions.com
ISBN 978-1-7332734-2-8
Design and composition by Crisis
Cover photographs by Juno Gemes: *Revelation at
Tea Tree Bay, NSW* and *Silver Gulls in the Light*
Printed in Canada

FOR JUNO GEMES

3

Robert Adamson has always been a restless poet, reinventing himself with each new book. As readers of this selection will find, his work abounds with redirections and experiments, from the nervy debut *Canticles on the Skin* (1970) through the bleak pared-down autobiography of *Where I Come From* (1979) to the rich and masterful late work. Yet through all the changes, a few place names recur like talismans, with their own particular weight and resonance. Returning to the same ground, the same waters, Adamson sifts through mysteries of the past, the traumas and "shining incidents" that accrete through long association. As Robert Creeley has written, he is "that rare instance of a poet who can touch all the world and yet stay particular, local to the body he's been given in a literal time and place."

For most of Adamson's life, his literal place has been the Hawkesbury River, an estuary just beyond the incursion of Sydney suburbs, even now. He and his wife, the photographer Juno Gemes, live in a house on the end of Cheero Point, outside the little town of Brooklyn. Their kitchen windows look out on Mooney Mooney Creek— really a broad river—which meets the larger body of the Hawkesbury a little south. Subject to tides, the creek withdraws to reveal mudflats, and sometimes its channel carries a bloom of jellyfish or a bull shark. Pleasure crafts mix with fishing boats, old oyster leases with freshly built jetties. The far shore remains wild, much as it would have looked to Governor Phillip in the late eighteenth century, with sandstone escarpments rising above inlets of mangroves and thick, low vegetation. It is part of Ku-ring-gai Chase National Park, named for the Aboriginal people who once lived here. Nearby runs the Great North Road, hewn from solid rock by convicts in the 1820s and 30s. The forces of the continent's history and prehistory are scratched on Hawkesbury stone, as colonial graffiti and Aboriginal petroglyphs. Such forces linger behind Adamson's writing, slightly inflecting poems of an otherwise personal nature and occasionally, as in "Wild Colonial Boys" and "Canticle for the Bicentennial Dead," coming into full view.

Near the creek's mouth, on the peninsula of Mooney Mooney, Adamson's grandfather "Fa Fa" lived in a cottage and fished the river for almost half a century. Adamson often sought refuge here, as a troubled youth growing up on the shores of Sydney Harbour. He felt alienated from the suburban, workaday world of Neutral Bay, and dyslexia hampered his progress in school. Meanwhile, as he recounts in his autobiography *Inside Out*, his grandfather taught him to "read" the river and advised him, "never stay away too long." As Adamson later reflected, "I grew up fishing on the Hawkesbury River and during those early years it seeped in, beyond the reach of conscious memory. Once it's in your blood it enters your life and you are governed by the tides, the fauna and flora, the mangroves and mudflats." In later years he made his living for a while as a commercial fisherman, and he has been a regular contributor to *Fishing World*. In poetry, the river has given Adamson not only subject matter, but also a rich vocabulary and symbolic language.

Throughout Adamson's poetry, fishing offers a figure for casting out into the landscape, drawing a line taut and reeling it in. The enterprise involves reading the tides and weather, an intimate familiarity with shifting conditions; like poetry, it combines technical facility, preparation, and good instincts. It entails intuiting a presence where nothing is visible, a sort of *via negativa*. In "Meaning," a fishing net becomes the web in which he seeks to catch his own memories: "tonight I work with holes, with absence." In the process, he moves not only outward but downward to psychological and instinctual depths. As he reflects in an article for *Fishing World*, "Memory is an active part of fishing, not simply the recording of facts but the deeper upper reaches of the subconscious river, the places where we once had to fish to survive." Yet fishing brings with it a deep ambivalence, since what we catch we usually kill; it taps sources of guilt as well as joy. In poems of love and loss, mulloway, hairtail, ribbonfish, catfish, black fish, leatherjackets, whiting, and bream glide through a psychogeography. In the reciprocity between outer and inner states, "the whole river, and the landscape around it, reflected what was happening in my head" (*Inside Out*). In a few poems, such as "The Gathering Light," ambivalence gets overwhelmed by a sense of awe:

> I've just killed a mulloway—
> it's eighty-five pounds, twenty years old—
> the huge mauve-silver body trembles in the hull.
>
> Time whistles around us, an invisible
> flood tide that I let go

while I take in what I have done.
It wasn't a fight, I was drawn to this moment.
The physical world drains away
into a golden calm.

Beyond the act of violence, beyond the workings of time and desire, Adamson arrives at a stunned surrender to the natural world.

Then, there are the birds that flock through Adamson's poetry, particularly from the 1990s onwards: whistling kite, Jesus bird, stone curlew, Arctic jaeger, yellow bittern, greenshank, rainbow bee-eater, too many to list here. For American readers, some of the very names may seem fantastical, and their sightings in these poems have surreal edges. Their songs and flight often bring a hint of euphoria, a flashing glimpse of alien life. They are always themselves, beyond anthropomorphic understanding, and never quite knowable in language. Yet paradoxically, perhaps, birds are also emissaries for poetry in Adamson's work. As Francis Ponge puts it, poetry takes "the side of things" (*Le parti pris des choses*), or in this case, the side of birds. It draws a larger circle within which human creativity and animal behavior are not cleanly separable. Playfully, the behaviors, codes, patterns, and ecologies of birds sometimes become those of poets. More earnestly, the kingfisher is Adamson's *daemon*, a fishing bird and deep diver. "It hunts / for souls," and yet "its life's / an edge / you can't / measure" ("The Kingfisher"). The entwining of wildness with literary sophistication proves one of many paradoxes in Adamson's work. Like that of Yeats, his poetry is shot through with paradoxes, ironies, antinomies, vacillation, and ambivalence, full of "straight, bent signs" ("Reaching Light").

We return often in these poems to a central tension between imagination and the real, between far-flung correspondences with art and poetry and everyday struggles, between resonances of myth and things as they are. The river flows through both worlds, sometimes as the Styx or Helicon, sometimes as the real Hawkesbury, but always the dark source of language and reverie. Its black water is often described as ink, the fluid substance in which poems get inscribed. Orpheus, in particular, recurs from the late 1990s onwards as a figure for the poet, sometimes appearing in murkily displaced autobiography during a period of personal turbulence. In the myth of Orpheus and Eurydice, he seeks to bring lost love up from the darkness into the light. Yet the backward glance precipitates loss at the very instant it seeks affirmation. As with fishing, the myth emphasizes evanescence, the limits to what we can grasp in love. Sometimes, as in "Eurydice in Sydney" and "Reaching Light," Adamson moves past this double bind by giving voice to the loved one, who has been nearly silent through the whole course of literature.

At other times, more oppressively, the space of imagination is a "head space." Bunkered at the back of the house, shades drawn against the daylight, the poet writes through the night, scattering words as "bait" for poems, until he feels a "strange panic / for the real" ("Clear Water Reckoning"). The head is invariably dark, a cave or refuge or confinement, at once boundless and claustrophobic. In "The Floating Head," he turns off the lights, unplugs the phone, "wrapped a scarf around my headache / and looked inside." He invokes the death of Orpheus as a self-mocking image of the poet's martyrdom: "I scribble // a few lines, pass my fishing rod off / as a lyre. Who needs this bitter tune?"

Writing poetry is a solitary activity, of course, and sometimes an isolating one. Yet with bookshelves close at hand, the poet finds company (to use Creeley's word) with the living and the dead. As we read in "Creon's Dream," "the dead friends sing from invisible books." Despite all the birds and fishes, Adamson's poems are highly literary. He has never been afraid of absorbing influences, having taken to heart Robert Duncan's celebration of "derivations" and joyful acknowledgment of sources. We can trace in Adamson's work the Romanticism of Wordsworth and Shelley, alongside the Symbolism of Rimbaud and Mallarmé (there are many French allegiances in Australian poetry of the 1960s, to tack against the English modes). Hart Crane is an early influence and presiding presence, along with the Australian poets Francis Webb and Randolph Stow. The Americans Duncan and Creeley were friends and correspondents, and their poetics gave Adamson an early whiff of freedom and possibility. On the level of form and style, Elizabeth Bishop and Robert Lowell can be felt, particularly the Lowell of *Near the Ocean* (1967), "crafting / lines of intelligent blues, / his Jelly Roll of a self-caught mess / deep in spiritual distress" ("Clear Water Reckoning").

These influences first took hold when Adamson was in his mid-twenties, a *poète maudit* recently released from a stretch in prison. He joined a blossoming counterculture in Sydney, including the poets of what came to be known as "the New Australian Poetry." Literature, Pop Art, and rock music mixed freely in the flats and hotel bars of Balmain and Paddington. In 1968 Adamson took over editorship of the Poetry Society of Australia's magazine, *New Poetry*, and edited it for more than a decade (and remained an editor of various publications, including Paper Bark Press, for the next thirty-odd years). He quickly took the magazine in an avant-garde direction, publishing some of the writing that defined his generation. His own early poetry often brings the cool of Jean-Luc Godard's *Bande á part* or Bob Dylan's *Blonde on Blonde* into verse. There's a thrilling insouciance evident from the outset: "Shit off with this fake dome of a life, why / should I remain here locked in my own / buckling cells?" ("The Rebel Angel"). Such toughness mingles with more vulnerable confessions and love lyrics. In some early poems, lines of free verse float like strands of cloud, sometimes underpunctuated. Elsewhere we find arch rhyming quatrains and sardonic sonnets. Arthurian legends mix with Customlines and Mallarméan poetics bump up against drug references.

Like many of his generation, a shocking number of whom did not reach middle age, Adamson struggled with addiction to drugs and alcohol. By *The Clean Dark*, published in 1989, we get a clear-eyed assessment of the damage done—clean now, but still dark. Adamson became, by force of circumstance, a fine elegist for lost friends, including the painter Brett Whiteley. The dark recognitions of a survivor blend with the pragmatism of a fisherman in poems such as "Windy Drop Down Creek," on Whiteley's death:

It was a blustering winter. I saw his name
in headlines, flapping outside a shop
next to the chemist. Death turns up
and life goes on incredibly, what can

you feel if the day turns to stone?

Heartbreak wells up in the midst of daily life, fully felt yet tersely expressed, without sentimentality. Death is a persistent presence in Adamson's major work from the late 1980s through the 1990s. Yet increasingly, in the last two decades, his poems have moved toward a tone of calm acceptance and plain statement, perhaps natural to late retrospection. In the recent poems for Juno Gemes, in particular, we find a hard-won sweetness and light. "I preferred the cover of night, yet here, I stepped / into the day by following your gaze" ("The Kingfisher's Soul").

For all of Adamson's exhilarating variety and intertextual play, certain features have emerged over time to define his strongest poems. He modulates between literary and spoken registers, high and low, with exquisite sensitivity. His poems are largely built up out of phrases that fall into syntactical arrangements with ease, their clauses strung together with commas, artfully yet without fuss. Their tones adhere closely to those of talk, either to himself or to a loved one. The poems rarely make arguments, usually beginning with seemingly casual observations that locate us in the day: "In small skiffs before dawn" ("Berowra Waters"), "Morning before sunrise" ("Green Prawn Map"), "Winter afternoon" ("Ambivalence"),

"Morning shines on the cowling of the Yamaha" ("The Gathering Light"), or "A black summer night" ("Meaning"). In this respect, they sound occasional, attentive as they are to the present moment. Yet line by line, such poems build toward memorable statements of clinching power.

Devin Johnston

1

THE REBEL ANGEL

Shit off with this fake dome of a life, why
    should I remain here locked in my own
buckling cells? So there's always
    a way round the city mornings when parks
are lakes of smouldering green—
    & there's a way as you're blown along
by some black vision of a cop that's
    nagging inside your gut—
you know so well the way that'll carry you back:
    follow a railway line

studded with muck-green stations
    & bubblers spouting lukewarm water—No,
you've left it too late & now there's
    cold weather coming along &
a pile of junk in your brain—These days it's
    risky to drive after midnight.
It's slowing you down always looking behind
    all the time getting someone to pluck
down the blinds—So now as you spin
    through a drunk there's lots of reasons

why you have to stay put—reasons that say
    you can't piss off anymore from
serving two and a half years straight: of knowing
    it's lights out at ten every night, of knowing
the sleepless lays churning in your bunk
    until each counted dawn, of singing
without sound—I've looked around every inch
    of the jail & dug my own groove in yellow
sandstone, & searched without sleep
    & searched again

back on the street in the rain—searched for
    some kind of rebel angel,
        some kind of law.

Dirty hypodermics rattle in the glove box—
morphine flows over the top of your brain—
an artery collapses—migraine floats out of your eyes.
Alright, there'll always be glib explanations:
cashing in on experience again?

Don't be distracted now, watch the speedo,
plant your foot until the big V8 starts
to mainline juice straight from your cirrhotic
liver—let her go, the most fantastic demo ever.
Low-flying through suburban hills, taking

red lights at sixty-five, hoping for some brick-wall
overdose to bash your head against,
until a piston snaps its rings and cracks the block—
but there's only a missing spark and kick
back from screwing in the dark. Don't freak now,

come down slow with codeine phosphate;
speed as much as you like, just hang on
to your impetus and never use the brake.
Keep shooting and you'll find there's no right
side to the double yellow lines—Make sure

the windscreen's always clean, don't read traffic
signs unless you've passed them once before.
When the morphine goes to water, move on
with heroin—shoot up with quality.
Stay clear of bike-boys, hoods, and Chinamen—

use anything, stay numb as long as you can,
any pain now could be deadly, they'll sense it,
knife in, and you're gone—Care for your
Customline's your habit, and you're on your own.

TOWARD ABSTRACTION/
POSSIBLY A GULL'S WING

The most disconcerting feature is an absolute flatness
especially the sand. I've been here in love
and having passed the perfectly calm ocean had only
noticed the terns—If there was some way
back, some winding track to follow I'd possibly find
the elusive agents of creativity.

As now for instance, I am completely indifferent
to the sad way that fellow moves over the sand . . . Who?
Let's be pure in observation, let's drop opinions—
Look: he stops and, throwing off his towel,
runs into the surf, where stroking out he attracts the terns
that begin to curve above him.

Now look back to the beach. It is mid-winter.
The sand's deserted and eddies of wind-caught grit are left
to dance and fall unhindered. At the far end of the beach
is an object—a rifle, rusting. He comes out from
the surf, stubbing his toes, heading towards the place
where the rifle lies melting.

The sand whispers beneath his feet as he passes by the gun.
Dazed, he goes in no particular direction.
The surf rolls a dead tern onto the sand and he kicks it.
Its wings unfold like a fan, sea lice fall from the sepia
feathers and the feathers take flight.

FROM THE RUMOUR

everything's involving
freedom now   even the image of a bird's
            bone & feathers
cutting her cheeks
                the confusing use
of the word 'heart'

        as it moved across
her cold face back there everything's
                folding because
nothing rings true
            'I write because
I have to' Hart Crane has had his
    day & if my

        pen is to be my spokesman
a muse can't be created by
                the poem's process
    as Augustine
underlines my desire for her
            'circumcise
        the lips of my

mind & mouth   purify them
of rash speech & falsehood'
                    his law has been broken
            & truth spreads out
its great wings into rumour
        as my lovely

        source rides the mode
as Christabel is slowly washed aside by
                lapping tide
my freedom a need that follows
                    creeps from
the small of my spine & now
        marrow catching fire as bones
support   support

        my freedom
extending from a crushed cloudy gown
            she wears as a joke
source after reoccurring
                    source in rumour
        I admire so much
before it's even half complete works on
            me every

time something confronts
                containing desire
    & I find myself
        practising a 'delicate' loneliness
then I'm caught in talk
                holding my household
posture in tow

        rumour proposed as television's
blue light showered us
                reoccurring source
after source as the idea of feathers
        falls flat nothing
more than another
            image pushed through
from the start

as the poem drags another stanza
                    from rumour's pulse 'without
    a plan I was destined to
come to this foreclosing
            of all promise'   so rumour
resolution's false

    a feather falls from
the bird when it is

perfectly conceived   the bird
          falls on a rodent
as viciously   one
          feather less

MONDRIAN: LIGHT BREAKS
UPON THE GRAIL

The skiff carelessly up against rocks
oysters   cleaning the fish   mosquitoes
on my thighs as I crouch in mangroves
silted roots force themselves

up into air   consciousness
seeks form here   shape these lines
in your mind   solids set down
church built from the local sandstone

by the river in a dark corner
where blessed shadows have crept back
and forth for a century or more
so far from Piet's white room

arranged to display human order
fish-knife sparkles in sunlight
tide-line junk shows even here
how they've smeared his pure contemplation

tobacco packet's lettering
red with heavy black rules—

Sun dries fish blood on arms
shirt and the clockwork of fishing tackle

my skiff up against the rocks   climbing
through swamp mahogany trees
sharp air to brace wounded lungs
stumbling into dry bracken

my eyes lining things up
strange to seek form here
consciousness is its own place   too late
the red bottlebrush shakes with honeyeaters

SIBYL

Then with my white sails and bad luck
with the wind I am beautiful
each dawn there is more resentment toward me fishermen
cannot look as the sun
catches my hair turning spokes
on their decks

So again I depart from the side of the planet
the boy who sleeps with me
Why speak

BEROWRA WATERS

In small skiffs before dawn fishermen came
through the valley sliding over calm waters.
Thinking of their catch, the long silver
ribbonfish, I stooped carefully over
the river from a rotting jetty into silence
and mist. Campaigns rose from reflected stars,
our campaigns against the flags of heaven:
murder of sacred fishes, the destruction of trees.
Then I rose from my reflection also
heroic in silver victory—and on the jetty
my catch, white as the planets and shining there
as inconstant as prayer.

SONNETS TO BE WRITTEN FROM PRISON

for James Tulip

1

O to be 'in the news' again—now as fashion runs
everything would go for 'prison sonnets': I'd be on my own.
I could, once more, go out with pale skin
from my veritable dank cell—the sufferer, poking fun
at myself in form, with a slightly twisted tone.
My stance, ironic—one-out, on the run.
Though how can I? I'm not locked up: imagine a typewriter
in solitary. I dream my police unable to surrender—
I'm bored with switching roles and playing
with my gender; the ironies seem incidental, growing thin.
Here's the world—maybe what's left of it—
held together by an almost experimental sonnet.
Surely there must be some way out of poetry other than
Mallarmé's: still life with bars and shitcan.

2

Once more, almost a joke—this most serious endeavour
is too intense: imagine a solitary typewriter? Somehow
fashion runs its course: I am not in pain,
so there's hardly any need to play on abstract repetitions

to satisfy a predecessor, poet, or lawbreaker. I won't be clever—
all the clever crims are not inside the prisons.
Here's the world—maybe what's left of my pretences:
I dream of being carried off to court again,
a sufferer, where all my deities would speak in stern
almost sardonic voices: 'Your Honour, please,
bring me to my senses'. There, I love confessions—
imagine writing prison sonnets four years after my release.
If only all my memories could be made taciturn
by inventing phrases like: imagine the solitary police.

3

Yes Your Honour, I know this is ridiculous—although
I'm 'in the news'. I couldn't bring myself to do
one of those victimless crimes: I must suffer in more ways
than one. My crime's pretence is not to overthrow
social order, or to protest—it's my plan
to bring poetry and lawbreaking into serious interplay.
Imagine newspapers in solitary. I would walk right through
the court taking down copy—'catch me if you can'—
Defendant in contempt. There has to be a fight,
I can't imagine anything if I'm not up against a law.
Here's the world—our country's first stone institution—
where inmates still abase themselves each night.
If I was in solitary I could dream—a fashionable bore,
writing books on drugs, birds, or revolution.

4

I dreamed I saw the morning editions settle on the court
emblazoned with my name, my 'story' so glib it made
no sense. The judge said 'emotional' but I thought
of the notoriety. This was the outward world and my sad tirade
was news—Though if I'd been rhyming sonnets
in solitary, my suffering alone could've made them art.
Now, imagine an illiterate in prison—but I have no regrets,
I enjoy my laggings. I feel sorry for the warders.
The discipline always pulls me through, and my counterpart,
the screw, is tougher with the easy boarders—
This experience might feel profound, but irony's never
broken laws—so I'm against everything
but practical intuitions. My 'solitary etc.' is too clever
by half now—but then, who's suffering?

5

I brood in solitary, it's a way to flagellation: thinking
of my 'day of release'—I shuffle friends like dates
on my calendar, marking them off at random.
Here's the world—the stewed tea I'm drinking
cold—how I suffer. When I walk through the front gates
into the country, what will I become?
I'll throw away the sufferer's comforting mask
and turn against my memories, leaving a trail of perdition

behind me. Children and women will fall to my simple
intuitive reactions—not even the New Journalists will ask
questions, nothing will be able to feed on
my actions and survive. My prison sonnets will be drugs
relieving pain: I have remembered helpless men
knocking their bars for hours with aluminium mugs—

6

We will take it seriously as we open our morning paper.
Someone's broken loose, another child's been
wounded by penknives. A small fire down the bottom
of a suburban garden smells of flesh. Dark circles under
the mother's eyes appear on television, she's seen
her baby at the morgue. Our country moves closer to the world:
a negro's book is on the shelves. The criminal's become
mythologized, though yesterday he curled
over and didn't make the news. So the myth continues, growing
fat and dangerous on a thousand impractical intuitions.
The bodies of old sharks hang on the butcher's hooks.
In broad daylight somewhere a prisoner is escaping.
The geriatrics are floating in their institutions.
The myth is torn apart and stashed away in books.

SOME MORE EXPERIENCES

Seems we were born in captivity, he said, and burn
Our curious lives out in these slow states
Numbered by the days; who knows? My lover's turn-
Coat mind turns about, dreaming of the gates.

And he forgets me easily behind the yellow walls.
He's been round on the outer—screws
Tell me he's even got a wife who calls
The Commissioner every day for some news

Of his release. (As if they'd know—
They bitch me many ways.) All night he talks
And holds me, all night he loves me slow
And careful. The screws pace the catwalks—

In time their footsteps mark our love.
Who, now, can really know him more than me?
Once he hugged me till my bones were sore—
We understood the terror then in being free.

Seems we should be born in captivity, I said; love
Might hold our curious lives in some new lore.
Oh, yeah, he said, whatever you reckon—
Love's a laggin' in a way, whatever you reckon.

THE BEAUTIFUL SEASON

Some sunny day does not support more
reason than a dull one; green lights
from the harbour still remind us of a tour
through Spain. Two whistling kites

are fishing in a shallow day: even birds
would not support a proper reason
for the inclusion of corroborated words.
A sample of the beautiful season

came wrapped in aluminium foil: oh cute
as a new drug—but let's remember
how the most vicious thug wore silk suits
and plugged sparrows in December.

The sunny day is no more 'cute' than a drug
in foil; lights on water are seldom
memories. Our bird-loving thug
has returned muttering 'O Kingdoms'

THE CROSSING

for Cheryl

Below full tide the catfish swim
long dark ribbons moving

slowly over the empty oysters—
From the house, where you

are waiting up, a clock's moving
against me—Only hours apart

and mathematics divide us.
When I return and hold you again

finally there will be sleep;
just to stroke your hair

would make the coldest planet relent.
Then we will watch the sun rise

washing the night's work
from my eyes, outshining

the sharp morning star: awakening
we'll see ourselves again

and taste the brackish river on
our lips: full morning

will soothe storms in your eyes,
as I tried during the night.

Though what can I offer? you,
from another river, what desire?

I have never tried to bless you,
though have wanted you here

each night, as the crossings bless
me—the river difficult

to navigate, and the tides
against me with a terrible patience.

I belong to you, now let nothing
divide us, even this.

A NEW LEGEND

In a friendless time the mind swims
out from its body: you become
all the lives you have ever lived.
In this clearing there have
been camp fires, though the ashes
are stone cold now. And the mist
just above the earth is
undisturbed. A brown kestrel flits

between the sun and the ancient
dwellings, its shadow a moth
wandering below the mist's surface.
Everything has been like this
for centuries. Sunlight struggles
through onto the petrified
branches of charcoal; as I walk
I create a new legend here—

my voice moves over the rock carvings,
my hands net for the moth's
faint dancing shadow, my eyes
vanish into the back of my head
and a small creature stops running.

The water lies still in granite
waiting for the chance to sing anew;
under the mist I become

a thousand echoes, sounding for
the time being. Wherever life emanates
it's born from my careful presence
here, treading: mushrooms bloom
in my footsteps among the ashes.
The mind moves ahead of my
body now, feeling the new wings,
wondering if they existed before.

Its thoughts lift me above the ground.
I look down at my body, a feeble
creature moving through its own silence.
Moss clings to my thighs, the kestrel
dives into the clearing hooking
up the creature I taught not to fear.

THE GHOST CRABS

I flow back into myself with tide.
O moon that draws us and drives
us and we move through until we are
dancing. Balancing starlight on
the marshes, shaking the leaves
or calming the water. Feeling warmth,
ghost crabs come out, their claws
snapping held high in the air.

The river pulls at mangrove roots
as the ebb begins: standing to
my waist in water, prawns kick up
from under my toes—My love
would have me go now—moving off
with the river, skidding along
beneath the silt, head filled with
water. Now flexing my limbs,

the shock of feeling comes back
to my nerves: memories play
their part again. Swamp flowers are
opening, ready for sunlight,
vines twine closer to their branches

and a kingfisher ruffles its feathers
against the dew. She beckons from
the far shore, a chill runs

along my arms—I wade into shallows
calling, and straining my sight.
She moves there through the mist,
dancing and calling softly, hardly
moving the vegetation. My hands
shoot out over the tide, gleaming as
fish in a soft light. The senses
strain forward towards claws

turning and growing from the dawn.
I cannot reach, hands drift
down through the moonlight onto the
outgoing tide. Morning surrounds
me silently, sun hitting driftwood,
dead roots and branches.

THE RIVER

A step taken, and all the world's before me.
The night's so clear

stars hang in the low branches,
small fires riding through the waves of a thin atmosphere,

islands parting tides as meteors burn the air.
Oysters powder to chalk in my hands.

A flying fox swims by and an early
memory unfolds: rocks

on the shoreline milling the star-fire.
Its fragments fall into place, the heavens

revealing themselves
as my roots trail

deep nets between channel and
shoal, gathering in

the Milky Way, Gemini—
I look all about, I search all around me.

There's a gale in my hair as the mountains move in.
I drift over lakes, through surf breaks

and valleys, entangled of trees—
unseemly? *On the edge or place inverted*

from Ocean starts another place,
its own place—

a step back and my love's before me,
the memory ash—we face each other alone now,

we turn in the rushing tide again and again to each other,
here between swamp flower and star

to let love go forth to the world's end
to set our lives at the centre

though the tide turns the river back on itself
and at its mouth, Ocean.

SUNLIGHT, MOONLIGHT

Out of a dying out of a death a new life shoots
Tide's deeper tension singing under the sapwood rockers
Sunlight through the smokehouse smoulders
Dry ice under canvas   mould eats the boathouse chaff bags
There's a familiar smell   of tar on the breeze
And the winter mullet too early in the season
Always slow and always now
The punishing fear of isolation
Winter nights dark with Eros taunting in the form of
Ribbonfish dancing   away within a tempest
And native doves   tumbling   swung
By fire and harsh summer   through these
Ancient signatures on rock

With each thing energy with each object each one
With the power to change
Energy the sunlight energy the panic
In doves in branches energy
And from the eyes

It was the river gathering in throughout
My forming limbs a feline sense
That tore down sexual boundaries in that
Separating light

I knew quicksilver and the darker water birds
And showered at the base of a mountain
Where water fell through mangroves

Winter warmed my nakedness
Seasons passed within my passing year
Cold desires rapt my heart and I bore twin anima

THE HEAVEN, THE OCEANS

The dice cast shall never, even through eternity,
spin off its true numbers.
Accounting even for the chance

of tides wrecking his ship, the gambler
navigates through each instant's circumstance.

Out over the calm harbour
out through the river's mouth

travelling beyond his domain, the skipper
inclines to the particular,

charts and instruments, charms
against instinct.

He gazes at you through his crazed eye

with an invitation to ride out a chance of storm.
Master of the high sea.

Though don't be curious,
don't wonder where you are.

These rituals becalm him, become habits
circling the memory.

The old sailor takes up his role and plays it out.
All the finer details,

the silver in his curls
and the days and nights at the helm,

appear where the dice might fall, his number up.
He could never let go

without his charts,
and glide over the altering tide to discover chance

an illusion.

It's a calm day, some cloud on the horizon
and the heat oppressive.
There's no way to see

this point in time, only the sun

rising above the cloud line

and we're sailing straight into it.

It has taken so much effort to break away;

there's history for you,
the journey a system of belief

our direction plotted out, a proposition
described on a stellar chart.

As if skill alone could guide us through disbelief.
The whole thing abstract.

DEAD HORSE BAY

Quick hands on spinning ropes
at dawn, blood rising
to the jumping cords,

icepacks over bad burns
and the catfish venom,
rock salt against gut-slime,

a southerly blowing up
on the full tide, nets
in mud and mesh-gutting snags,

the bread tasting
like kero-sponge, crazed gulls
crashing onto the stern

and mullet at three cents a pound
by the time the sun hits the bar
at the Angler's Rest.

Get drunk enough to keep at it,
clean the gear for tonight
and another bash.

Remember that night in '68
how we killed 'em
right through the month,

couldn't have gone wrong,
so thick you could've
walked over the water.

When the bream are running
like that, nothing can touch you
and everything matters

and you don't want 'em to stop
and you can't slow down
you can't imagine.

THE MULLET RUN

Gone for days, and way down the river—
an old man? We sat around the Angler's Rest
playing the jukebox: Slim Dusty
saving us from talk. I played with my

rum & Coke. We were home by midnight, walked
all the way to Mooney, and Christ,
where was he, as if I didn't know. I slept on
the verandah to overlook a slackening tide.

3 a.m. my cousin came back to say
she loved me—soon I would explore my sensual
dream, and Sandy's beery breath—like
I'd planned all those months. A southerly,

of course, blew up just before dawn, ripping
canvas from the window frames; branches
snapped clean off the mulberry tree
to fall across the bed. Our calico

sheets were soaked with rain and sticky dark
stains. Almost half the rusty
corrugated iron blew from the roof,
and, really, what could've I done? Wind dropped,

dawn, sun in the slanting mulberry tree.
It was midday before our grandfather
finally got back. We heard his boat down beside
the wharf—I stayed in the house

pretending to clean up. By the time he came
through the front door, saw the roof half gone,
and said there'd been a mullet run,
we knew somehow he didn't want to know.

I couldn't have told him then, but needed him
to ask. We just followed him down
to his trawler, helping to pack mullet into
boxes of crushed ice. Sandy was the first to go,

she just dropped everything and ran.
I knew he didn't really want me there,
but held on for a while at any rate—and then
filled a kero tin with mullet gut,

carried it up the yard, and sat there an hour
feeding it to his chooks. The scales curling in the sun,
falling from my arms.

ON SATURDAYS

I'd walk with Sandy to town
so Mr Darcy could see us

holding hands and kissing

we'd pinch bottles of his oysters
and take them to the pictures
and eat them out of each other's mouth
or spit them down our shirts

We thought we had probably
committed mortal sin even more times
than Mandy Kerslake

I'd tell Sandy stories about
what hell was like

it was one great mudflat
and our punishment would be to
suck out each other's eyes

MY FIRST PROPER GIRLFRIEND

The first girl I wanted to marry
was Joan Hunter
her father owned more oyster leases
than anyone else on the river

she had buck teeth
but she looked okay really

we'd sit on her father's wharf
and watch the mullet together for hours

they will take over the world one day

we loved each other alright

my parents hated us being together
and called her Bugs Bunny

One night my father cut Joan's dad
with a fishing knife
right down his left cheek

that little Protestant bludger
with his stuck-up bitch of a daughter

THE HARBOUR BRIDGE

I went with Dad on the sulky
into town across the Harbour Bridge

it was a windy cold day

I wasn't too keen on going
along in a horse and cart in the city

I slid down under the seat
so the horse's tail swished in my face

we passed trams and women
standing at the crossings

and Dad just driving through it all
as if he was still up the river

his hat on his head
and his son beside him
with the city grit getting on me

the shopping growing in the back
beans and tomato trees

the blood and bone spilling behind us

MY HOUSE

My mother lives in a house
where nobody has ever died

she surrounds herself
and her family with light

each time I go home
I feel she is washing
and ironing the clothes of death

these clothes for work
and for going out
to the Club on Sunday
and for Jenny to take her baby
to the doctor in

death comes on the television
and Mum laughs

saying there's death again
I must get those jeans taken up

MY GRANNY

When my granny was dying
I'd go into her bedroom
and look at her

she'd tell me to get out of it
leave this foul river

it will wear you out too

she was very sick
and her red curly hair
was matted and smelt of gin

sometimes I sat there all day
listening to the races
and put bets on for her at the shop

and I sat there the afternoon
she died and heard her say her last words
I sat there not telling

maybe three hours
beside the first dead person I'd seen

I tried to drink some of her gin
it made me throw up on the bed
then I left her

she said the prawns will eat you
when you die on the Hawkesbury River

MY FISHING BOAT

Mum and Dad are at it again
in the room
next to mine
their terrible sobbing
comes through the damp wall

they fight about something
I have done

I get out of bed
and go down the yard to the river
push my boat out into
the black and freezing bay

under the mangroves
that smell like human shit

I move along my secret channel
my hands blistered
from rowing slip with blood
around the cove I tie up on a mangrove
it rains harder

all I catch are catfish here
and have them sliding
about in the belly of the boat

they are the ugliest-looking things
in the world

FROM GROWING UP ALONE

Fishing skiff in the light
at Mackerel Flats, mud-caked, sun borne
by the old man caulking cracks.

Rust scales drop from boat slip
to silt as he moves.

Gnawed, hacked heads of black bream
rock through the wash.

Skeleton trophies, banjo rays,
staked out on a pile,
their whip tails paralysed chalk.

Light seeps through folds in his turkey neck—
his eyes don't blink

and flick out involuntarily to where
mud-gudgers pick at the heads.

He is alone with his tinkering work.

He holds the scraper
like a little axe and chips
away at the belly of his boat,

his finger flesh grown over
his fingernails, his hair freckled white,
his pupils contracted points.

It is morning
and the mangrove air is sweet

as I move toward him, my leather shoes
cracking oyster grit.

I ask how's the fishing,
my alien voice reminding me
he is the grandfather of what I am.

MY AFTERNOON

I think of sex all afternoon

it becomes memory
the wide beds
and the fleshy women

who got me here

the mornings are best
spent alone
I can't do anything in the mornings
with women any more

I am taken from place to place
as I pretend
to be good about sex

then quite drunk
I lie back in the folds
of their particular sheets

face buried in fear near shame

RIMBAUD HAVING A BATH

To have been held down in a park
the animal breath on your face
hands tightening on the throat
grappling at you in the dark

A life lashing out to embrace
the flesh and green bones under it
and then the infected slime
injected by the half-erect cock

remains a flesh wound until
morning and poetry begin their work
in the carnage under the skull
The great poet goes home again

to his mother and becomes
the boy he is and feels the pain
subside his senses numbed
by the fire boiling the water
and the yellow soap in the copper

He takes a rag and pumice stone
and slides his naked body in
Because he has taken this bath
he has betrayed his art having washed
the vermin from the body and the heart

MORNING KISS

I woke and thought to turn
our hi-fi on, then
wanted to be there,
between the speakers, with you—
It might turn out to be
the day rock music lets us
down. There
can be no thought
more black, nothing blacker
to think of or remember,
I thought to myself
and was once more, about you,
utterly wrong.

THE HOME, THE SPARE ROOM

I am the poet of the spare room
the man who lives here

with television's
incessant coloured noise

between the ads keeping the children
at bay

At night I walk the seagrass
down the hall

my head rolls before me
like some kind of a round dice

which room tonight?

I think of my wife-to-be
who has thrown herself down

in a foetal shape onto her bed

I am a hard man, a vicious seer
who simply wants

to go on living—love is beyond me

if it exists—my heart,
so called, is as efficient as a bull's

and as desperate
for the earth's treasures—

I turn into the spare room
and begin to write a poem of infinite

tenderness

IN THE NIGHT

The sheets are wrapped about me
I wake in a bad mood
You stand in the centre of it
It's been four days since I was with you
now you enter my dreams
in the same mood as I left you
petulant your head in
some old tantrum
I untangle myself and get up
then walk out into the dark house
my feet pad the cold
once again I hear the empty words
repeating promises vows a pledge
impossible charms against age and despair
We have all our lives left to live through
why must we watch ourselves
here in the present repeating our
selves our love hopeless
We hack away at our heads
our faces tense rubbing in the salt
our skin drawn the top lips
hanging loose
We have made the rendezvous

though each time we meet and touch
is another wound that will not heal
Why do we insist on being
real this way there is
a life each day the colours
surround us and at night we work
or sleep between television
and the bright moments of solitude
strange dreams of courage
I reach the kitchen moonlight
the smell of cooked meat
the luminous circle of the stove clock
I turn and go back into
the living room
my family is sleeping I sit at my desk
and stare at the blue machine
In your house across the harbour
you wake turn on your side and curse me
Okay call me a ghost of a man

GLASS BAY SONNETS

I wanted you to know all about my new life
wondered what you would think of it
waiting here at the gates of hell
the stove burning the breakfast toast
another morning scraping away
in the hedge-lined garden where the petals
of the black-eyed susan have fallen
like orange moths along the path

I wanted you to see for yourself what you
were not missing out on these days
though I knew you would be thinking of me
cool underneath the peppermint tree
looking out across the bay at the seagulls
raking the tide for whitebait

Well yes my kitchen window does look over
Glass Bay and the parrots chatter
through the bushy trees their sheen of
flashy colour bright in the green foliage
at night the flying foxes climb in the figs
the darkness is so calm I sleep again
I have discovered the secrets
of description by simply living here

Only yesterday three great black cockatoos
came swooping into our garden
we gave them bread and nuts to eat
their screeching terrified the cat so much
she sprang up onto the terrace
a frenzied ball of fur in the potted geraniums

I climbed to calm her and she hissed and spat
and clawed my arm across a vein
and though I pulled back quickly there was
blood in the kitchen and a tea towel streaked
trails splattering across the floor
the severed vein gushing into the sink
swirling with tap water and stale tea-leaves
I was so astonished I felt no pain

I know it's nothing to write home about
though I try sitting here surrounded by a view
where the bay ebbs and the gulls squabble
in the wash for the dead and injured bait
and a yacht its sail a membrane that trembles
with light pulls out from the marina

BEYOND THE PALE

for Tim Storrier

The certainty of it all, as clear as clear water,
like the sky a thousand miles out
into the desert, the complex distances
between horizon and sun. The expectation
of solitude, alive with reds
and the wild desert blues, with light
sinking into anything that stands upright.

On the way we notice coloured ensigns
emblazoned onto the windows
of the final service stations—winged horses,
golden rams, scallop shells; the night neon
pulsing through their skin.
I remember you saying something like:
'if a thing is made well enough,
it has a soul, the craft itself imparts
the craftsman's.' I looked again—the soul
of a glass scallop?—then marvelled
at your carpenter's trust for the next fifty miles.

At dawn the landscape we sailed through
became horizontal, we passed the ruined craft
of wrecked houses, destroyed fences
and random posts leaning at angles
into the gnarled scrub. We looked straight
ahead, in silence, wanting to talk,
though not of this desert junk. Is the stump
the indigenous art of this scene, pole,
post, and pale—necessity? A totem
that can both dispel fear of the dark, night—
then by day embellish itself
with the refractions of sunlight passing through
the atmosphere.

Outside we noticed the convex distance
shimmering into sky, the road flying
into it, an Egyptian measuring ribbon.
Soon our reckoning and what we have
imagined will meet out here, at some
ground zero of time, beyond the shadow sticks
of palings—on a plateau of light
so brilliant not even tone could forge
its tricks with shape. Now earth rushes
on all sides, we take bearings from each other;
a half-completed phrase, eyes sliding aside,
awkward gestures. The signs we make

signifying our ease with the interior life,
the privacy of art. We smell the motor labouring
on the invisible slope. Everything
that appears makes us think of permanence;
our heads imagining two flecks of onyx
moving across this waste of light.

Our campsite appears to vibrate
in the sunlight, we move under the canvas
shades and look out to the horizon. We create
signs then stake lives on them—signs
can't be constant in themselves, like tokens, chips
of black opal, flung into the sun's abyss.
There's no future other than oblivion
for our signs and their dogged followers.

I scratch some lines onto a rock with the chalky
femur of some perished marsupial—then confide
in you—'These are runes.' You turn calmly
and concur with, 'Then they are' . . .
and my head fills with dismay.
So the only permanence is in what we
say, what we imagine through language,
a permanence neither within nor beyond the pale.
The fine and burning line of art, the fence.

LANDSCAPE

The grey wharf creaks under my weight
maybe a hundred years
since these piles were driven in
and the planks laid across
The river moves slowly over mudbanks
swallows dive and glide through clouds
of white ants in the low sky
I take my fishing rod in my hands
shift weight onto one leg
and cast the bait in a long and graceful arc
It splashes beside an old snag
I look across the river at a derelict house
its for-sale sign askew
on the paling fence and the garden
a bush of rusted wire in the yard the great
hulk of a wrecked Chevrolet

2

GREEN PRAWN MAP

in memory of my grandfather H. T. Adamson

Morning before sunrise, sheets of dark air
    hang from nowhere in the sky.
No stars there, only here is river.

      His line threads through a berley trail,
a thread his life. There's no wind
    in the world and darkness is a smell alive

    with itself. He flicks
a torch, a paper map *Hawkesbury River*
    & District damp, opened out. No sound
but a black chuckle

    as fingers turn the limp page.
Memory tracks its fragments, its thousand winds,
    shoals and creeks, collapsed shacks

a white gap, mudflats—web over web
    lace-ball in brain's meridian.
This paper's no map, what are its lines

as flashlight conjures a code
from a page of light, a spider's a total blank?
So he steers upstream now

away from map-reason, no direction to take
but hands and boat to the place
where he will kill prawns, mesh and scoop

in creek and bay and take
his bait kicking green out from this translucent
morning.

Flint & Steel shines
behind him, light comes in from everywhere,
prawns are peeled alive.

Set rods, tips curve along tide, the prawns howl
into the breeze, marking the page.
He's alone as he does this kind of work—

his face hardened in sun, hands
moving in and out of water and his life.

FULL TIDE

My whole being's the bay,
cradled in the warm palm
the steady open hand of today's
flood tide. Anyway
let's tell the fishermen
something they already know—
it's the fabled calm
before the flow: I love
a gypsy with a lithe
soul who's difficult to please.
So may the resonance
of this new psalm begin life
here, then moon-change
phase to phase—it's fishermen
who recognize my strength,
who say to keep an eye
on me, then look long
at her art, sense vision's
power—the dance,
intellect and body, her total
elegance. Ah river
with ageless dreams, sorceress
with sea hawks and gliders,

updrafts in phosphor-fire, eyes
quick for your lips, thighs—
speak, tell me fables
as you flow. Ah tide that stops
dead, for my wild Magyar—
genuflecting from your ancient bed.

THE JESUS BIRD

The lotus bird's signature
is slenderness, moving

without ring-marking water's
skin-tight surface.

A colourist, strokes tone
with a wing, fans out pinions:

The show's to escape
death in shape of harrier

or swamp's light-slashing pike.
The night watch is a dance

where bird antenna
probes mind-stepping illusions

to parry with a stray
plug-throwing fisherman,

alert in thin air
whirred by a dragonfly's

cellophane propeller,
or puttering swamp bugs.

When the creek's back is dark
glass, a conjurer, stripper,

lotus-dancing with river-pimps.
Creek alley's sideshow.

WILD COLONIAL BOYS

Musk ducks and the plump Wonga pigeon
were knocked from the sky
in blood sport, left to rot, then afterwards
in firelight were the games,
all various forms of gambling. In the mist
you'd hear knucklebones rattle
in their cotton pockets or, darned
in conversation, obscene words, slurred
by badly brewed alcohol; never song
but garbled recitations, coughed half-chants.
Whatever fed the imagination
was like a yellowness: it showed
in various activities, from plucking
ducks to the way they slept in postures
of loose decadence. The river
was a flood of their refuse, a smear of thick
waste through the countryside. After
storms and at low tide you'd see the details
of their hate: the score, a tally, and what they called
their stake—the sacred remnants
of an ancient tribe's estate.

CANTICLE FOR THE
BICENTENNIAL DEAD

They are talking, in their cedar-benched rooms
on French-polished chairs, and they talk
in reasonable tones, in the great stone buildings
they are talking firmly, in the half-light
and they mention at times the drinking of alcohol,
the sweet blood-coloured wine the young drink,
the beer they share in the riverless riverbeds
and the backstreets, and in the main street—
in government-coloured parks, drinking
the sweet blood in recreation patches, campsites.
They talk, the clean-handed ones, as they gather
strange facts; and as they talk
collecting words, they sweat under nylon wigs.
Men in blue uniforms are finding the bodies,
the uniforms are finding the dead: young hunters
who have lost their hunting, singers who
would sing of fish are now found hung—
crumpled in night-rags in the public's corners;
discovered there broken, lit by stripes
of regulated sunlight beneath the whispering
rolling cell window bars. Their bodies
found in postures of human-shaped effigies,

hunched in the dank sour urinated atmosphere
near the bed-board, beside cracked lavatory bowls,
slumped on the thousand-grooved, fingernailed walls
of your local police station's cell—
bodies of the street's larrikin Koories
suspended above concrete in the phenyl-thick air.
Meanwhile outside, the count continues: on radio,
on TV, the news—the faces
of mothers torn across the screens—
and the poets write no elegies, our artists
cannot describe their grief, though
the clean-handed ones paginate dossiers
and court reporters' hands move over the papers.

REMEMBERING POSTS

for Manfred Jurgensen

In this country, beyond the sparkle
and the junk, the weekend blood
arenas, beaches full of paddlepops
and shit, out along the road
you stop noticing flags for hamburgers
or the empire, it all becomes a streak
of colour smearing the windscreen—
as you drift freeways or swerve
and loop down narrow passes you
realize you could be anywhere
in the world in your head, though
nowhere else you'd feel like this—
a passenger of memory floating out
across centuries. After distance
lulls you become a mobile antenna,
taking it in as each nerve flicks
with pain, sensing flesh wounds
in the open-cut mountainside, broken
bones under desert crust. Now you
know that if you stop you would shoot
roots and grow branches, leaves,

flowers—or you'd spear yourself
into the earth and sprout up
like a telegraph pole, a grey post
on the edge of a gibber plain, and be
stuck there swaying in the dry wind,
remembering.

AMERICAN SONNET

for John Forbes

I am the snow bandit who must travel
in the red-dirt night, this hat is
for style more than anything, shade
amuses me, or the idea of shade
I should say as no such thing exists
in the spirit world of talk. I wrestle
butterflies of light with my gaze,
these strange tracks that I leave
are for the anthropologist of morning;
ash fills my pockets as I fold away
sheets of anything resembling thought;
all I go by is the way it feels, no
thing bothers me unless it hurts.
I don't know what worship is for, let
alone what it is—I tried once in
swampland to the north of here to
describe talk, no such luck, no
such pain, yes even words perish
from lack of care, lack of use.

AN ELM TREE IN PADDINGTON

Branches of grapevine thick as ankles
grow through the terrace-iron,
the fruit is a bitter wood; I think

of Brennan standing on similar joinery,
in the same suburb, soured by love
and Symbolism. A black beetle waves

a feeler, its lasso, involves itself
with the security mesh before the panes
of rain-printed glass. I drink

American whisky from a champagne flute
and think of Lawson at the Rose & Crown,
he knew the price of a beer

cost more than the blackest sonnet.
The drinkers choose not to hear
parody in a voice, see the rag of a suit,

know the terrible hour it took
to shave up and comb for this sad front.
Out in the yard an old elm shoots

out from the acid dirt at an angle,
its boughs spokes of sylvan thought, here
where form eats content to a gloss.

COUPLETS

for Juno

On days still when the tide's full, river
hours with you are momentary fire

in the head, shall not stay memories
even, so intensely lived: just to sense

bay calm and watch the seconds scatter.
These cupped hands of brackish water

evaporate as light fragments in hair flicker
with mangrove's shade for your skin—

I know grassbanks where we rolled together
on the shaggy cotton-brush, now remember

not to remember any day other than our
morning on Jerusalem Bay, there as tide

turned the stern, our boat was afloat on a mist
rolling in, full of the song of the wattlebird.

SONGS FOR JUNO

1

My lies are for you, take them utterly, along
with the truth we are explorers for.
An old skiff mutters, pushes up Hawkesbury mud—
the image comes in, drifts, sinks, disappears:
shape-changing gods, we dream in separate bodies;
a part of it, we want feathers for sails;
the rivers we dance stand upright in the sky,
distance between them—though at headlands
fork, touching mix, become ocean.

2

Wind and the sails full in dreaming with you.
We talk of great deserts, old chalk cities,
ice language and its lava. Then imagination darts,
Tasmania appears filling our bedroom, sails
are wings of geese, homing ocean, white tricks
of the distance. How do we leave our tiny pasts?
My love, time fragments, blows into space—
we ride, fly, sail in every way we find there is
to now. Bring us a new language, to remake
these questions, into dream, the gale, I whisper
to you softly.

3

How long in these secret places from childhood—
the old embers smoulder on, the lowlands
laced with fire-lines, long spokes turning
in sky—were we at play—or were the games more
half-remembered charms, songs? We inhabit,
are rocked by still those innocent passions.
Dressed up for the new ritual, we move
the circle more than dance it. Take the moment,
hold it to you, the new, my brave and frightened
lover is a sacramental kiss. Our dreams touch—
warm with light. Give me your nightmares too.

4

Paint flaking from the belly of an old clinker.
The boys with their rods, prawns
and bloodworms rubbed through their hair,
tasting the westerly around Snake Island—
and you sleeping, curled around the stern.
The mountains everywhere, skirts of the mangroves,
then at Dangar's jetty, an octopus
sucking for its life at the end of a line.
Blue wrens hovering for invisible insects, a shag
hunched on a swing. The trim park
patched there amongst the scribbly gums,

houses, a wash-shed, and in a backyard
lemongrass drying in the sunlight.

5

The new list begins.

AS IMPERCEPTIBLY . . .

after Miklós Radnóti

Before you know it you're drifting off
in a dream, a kid again—
but then you wake, a man, to find
yourself staring down
a bottle of gin as you think
about your friends who've become
fathers. Then one of them
turns up with his son, a kid you
hit it off with, and play
with for years on the floor
as he senses your heart seared
by experience. Sometimes you even
manage to earn a man's wage:
you translate, sell a song; then
by hedging your bets, you make poetry
pay—although you don't flirt
with success, it doesn't hurt to
try it on, it makes sense,
it's like everything—
even your muse goes for a man
with good timing; of course you love

poppyseed, purple-fleshed
Black Forest cherries,
and not this honey-walnut cake
that all the smooth young men go for.
Yes you know the leaves
also fall in summer; and no matter
how much your brain, chopping
and changing, dancing and duping itself
tries to alter things,
it will all inevitably, after
you've gone, be weighed up as folly
by eternity's scales. You know
you'll never be an Olympian or a pirate,
though your pen's as much a weapon
as a tool; and if you play
a Stradivarius, it's neckbreaking
work, to create a state
where your willpower can live nakedly
in an atmosphere singed with sheer adventure.
Though as you lean on your pen
children come to mind,
and with no trace of conceit left
in your heavy heart, now you work for them—
in the same way the workers
in screeching factories work in silent dust,
their backs bent in the workshops.

CLEAR WATER RECKONING

I write into the long black morning,
out here on the end of the point,
far from my wife in Budapest—
as the river cuts through a mountain
in Sydney a poet is launching
his new volume *Under Berlin*
and I feel like Catullus on Rome's edge
but this passes and I turn to face
the oncoming dawn, the house
breathes tidal air as the night
fires outside with barking owls,
marsupials rustling, the prawn bird
beginning its taunting dawn whistle;
I burn the electricity
and measure hours by the lines—
I have strewn words around the living room,
taken them out from their
sentences, left them unused wherever
they fell; they are the bait—
I hunch over my desk and start to row,
let the tide flow in, watch
the window, with the door locked now
I wait—hear satin bowerbirds

scratching out the seeds from bottlebrush.
Dawn is a thin slit of illuminated
bowerbird blue along mountain lines,
in this year of cock and bull
celebration the TV goes on unwatched
upstairs, I hear it congratulating us
for making Australia what it is—
the heater breathes out a steady stream
of heated air—I go deeper
into my head, I see the Hawkesbury
flowing through Budapest, the Hungarians
do not seem to mind, they are bemused,
the river parts around their spires and domes,
I see other cities, whole cultures
drawn from territories within,
though with this freedom
comes a feeling of strange panic
for the real; so I get on
with it, writing out from this egg
holding my thought in a turbulent knot,
a bunched-up octopus. I steer
away from anything confessional,
thinking of Robert Lowell crafting
lines of intelligent blues,
his Jelly Roll of a self-caught mess
deep in spiritual distress.

Outside the river pulls me back,
shafts of light disintegrate into clues,
flecked symbols shine with order—
the bowerbirds have woven colour
around the house, through
bushes blue patterns of themselves
traced about the place; half
the moon can topple a mountain,
anything is possible here
I remind myself and begin to hum,
flattening out all the words that were
impossible to write today. I hum
out all the poems I should have
written, I hum away now also
the desire to write from memory—
there is enough sorrow in the present.
I look out over the incoming tide, dark racks
of oysters jut from its ink.

NO RIVER, NO DEATH

1

Awake after years: sudden exploding mangroves
alight as Mooney vanishes in mountain shade—

late afternoon, confusion of words, language
alive with a life of its own, lashing

out then licking its flesh wounds.
Words of the river, swarming in branches

of mangrove with prawn birds and fruit bats
and mullet butting upstream,

schooling, leaping,
and bull-nosed singing mullet songs—

silver green needs being spun till the spawn is done.

The river hawks tear at the heart's flesh, eat,
fly, in a moment's pocket of heaved air

where they are mullet's fear. Though here
on the tide's line, a torn wing of stingray

waves in wash, prawns fester on the underside.

2

Now leave from a jetty, souls going where souls go.
The world's a mudbank in a dank westerly

and there's nothing to hand, nothing to hold,
death's all around in the afternoon air.

Here with the spirits of river gods, the lost,
lost in a holy place, its histories

entangled with sadness, deep sorrow's
in the rotting and remembering.

Over this: planks, cut from swamp, return—
hewn from trunks in their green years

now creaking complainers in the dull sun.

The wharf sags with tar-drenched oyster racks
and a fisherman's punt rocks at its side for Charon.

3

Nets circle the mullet school, the fishermen
shake their mesh and the old rope stings

the stumped fingers and crooked thumbs,
then the fish buck under and die

in the net's wing-lock; like a cloak cast
out from the fishers' minds the green tide's

gone black and the mullet are done,
hauled to their death from the spawning run.

4

Now here in a creek on Mooney Bay all river
life calms the head that broods

on politicians oceans away, microwaved
down to our side of the planet,

their sickness infecting the silt of this tide.
They are death men rattling loaded dice,

war-headed malformations of the mind
as an eyeless reaper, its cloak space-fabric,

its titanium blade, its skull-powdering radium,
with the crippling power of crab-thought

turning its claws onto its own black flesh.

To feel it here with the ancient river
alive in a crawling

flying prehistoric line drawn on a rock—
here in the belly of the serpent's beginnings—

is to know we may not go where all souls go.

5

We live with the threat of that white flash
until again like hawks we gamble

with flesh, with oblivion—

and tear from the thin blue wind the black heart
of the cave our sick heads come from.

6

The afternoon's last light has gone under now.
A flying fox swims in through a star,

catfish are pecking the stingray's wing.
The larrikin prawn bird starts to sing.

ODE ON BECKETT'S DEATH

Take back the day though there's no
one to say that to

for I would give the day away
and let someone else spell out

words for the deal
and who's making it

no one can say
cleave these syllables

through the knot my tongue is
torn against the devil

who does not have to spell out
words bunged into words

grief yes give us grief for god's sake

WAVING TO HART CRANE

Farewell to the wire,
the voices on
the line. Goodbye
switchboard rider, my

American friend.
We enter the new
century through glass,
black oceans

and black winds,
thin fibre funnelling
poetry out
of existence.

No sonnet will survive
the fax on fire,
out-sound that hash
of voices slung up

from the cable.
Tip your hat
and flicker with
smoke from silent movies,

there are no more
cunning gaps left
on the cutting-room
floor by editors.

Here they expunge
the message, nothing's
praise. If gestures
appear they fold in fade-out.

FOLK SONG

for Kevin Hart

We live here by this
sliding water, brown by day,
black at night

flecked with bats
and the blue powdery stars.
Morning, a kingfisher

sits, an indigo rock
knife-shaped, winking
sun-speckled. There are too

many of us here,
still they keep coming,
rockets and landmines pock

their dreams. Here
the long-billed ibis go savage
in the mangroves:

Egyptians, blown in
on some cosmic whim, they
plunge their heads

into the black mud swamp
and drag out long bloodworms;
the royal spoonbills

shake their crowns,
head feathers white calligraphy
of surrender. We sing

of the mulloway, our
mauve-scaled river cod. They
rise breaking the surface,

our songs mention
mulloway kills and at night
we eat the rich cream-coloured flesh.

ROCK CARVING WITH
KEVIN GILBERT

The fish outlined on the rock
is the shape of a mulloway, we are moving
here under a fine yellow rain
pouring from the spear wound
in its side. A lyrebird dances above,
trembling the morning silk air.
We fish with two swamp harriers,
sweet whistling killers like us, who cut
fish throats and clasp up
bunches of silver nerves—
calling under stars convicts
hacked in the cliff face.
We crush oysters with rocks
and throw them as berley into the tide
we call our Milky Way.
After a while stingrays
come on the bite, then one after
another, brown-winged,
hump-backed, yellow-bellied
bull-rays fight to their death—
we cut some free to watch slide
over carvings of themselves,
back into the drink, as the rock mulloway
moves its shallowing grooves.

AMBIVALENCE

Winter afternoon
an hour before

low tide,
two fishermen

are meshing
for the mullet

they net all
the way around

an oyster lease.
One coughs

his death rattle
drifts across

the flat dark
surface. The light

fades and they
bash the bottom

of their boat
with an oar

and a wooden club,
thud, thud, cough

cough. I watch
the mullet

boil under corks
of their mesh net,

great fish-rings
run slowly

over the tide,
serifs of death.

ON THE ROCK

The black shag
oily cormorant

river bird
snake-necked

ordinary-looking
fish-killer

opens its wings
and holds them

to dry in a breeze
perfectly still

black flag
signs this day

with a smudge
on the bright sky

as it moves
on the opaque blue

between the relentless
tide and death's

chuckle while
life the old fisherman

like a dirty joke
in a sour pub

keeps repeating
these personifications

CORNFLOWERS

in memoriam Robert Harris

In a skiff, anchored
on the edge of a mangrove
swamp, he gave me

a version,
an unpolished song,
something that might have

gone unspoken
in our bright lives;
there is no dark side

he told me: things
will glow, sing, or die though
if we want them to,

it's all alive,
I just want to know who
owns the conversation

we may have some day, who
owns the dialogue
he repeated as

a flathead slapped
and shuddered
in the belly of the boat,

its pale speckles
flaring, the blue
barred tail fanning air,

who owns the words
as they hovered
with plump mosquitoes

and collided with
a whiting in flight
down a cadence of dancing

particles, our
hearts locked in their
cages of singing muscle;

it was concerning
this theme, he continued,
that I composed a tune

for the cornflowers
to sing, cut, sitting
on my table in an indigo jar.

THE KINGFISHER

after Montale

It hunts
for souls, he said
as I watched
it dive
from a wire
into
a mudflat
one second
then flash
indigo
between
leaves in
a mangrove tree,
its life's
an edge
you can't
measure,
it's an arrow
that goes
home unaimed.
These days

the weekend
fishermen
with their
depth-sounders
hardly
know what
a soul
might be
and yet they
are frightened
they might
somehow lose them.

MESHING BENDS
IN THE LIGHT

Just under the surface
mullet roll in the current;
their pale bellies catch
the sunken light, the skin
of the river erupts
above purling. The sky
hangs over the boat a wall
of shuddering light
smudging the wings
of a whistling kite,
mudflats glow
in the developing chemicals,
black crabs hold their
claws up into the light
of the enlarger, yabbies
ping in the drain. A westerly
howls through the
darkroom. The tide
is always working
at the base of the brain.
The turning moon is
up-ended, setting on the silver

gelatin page: a hook
stopped spinning in space.
Owls shuffle their silent wings
and dissolve in the fixer.
Shape words over what you see.
The river flows from your
eyes into the sink, bulrushes
hum with mosquitoes
that speckle the print.
The last riverboat mail-run
scatters letters across
the surface, the ink
runs into the brackish tide.

THE LANGUAGE OF OYSTERS

Charles Olson sat back in his oyster-shed
working with words—'mostly in a great
sweat of being, seeking to bind in speed'—

looked at his sheaf of pages, each word
an oyster, culled from the fattening grounds
of talk. They were nurtured from day one,

from the spat-fields to their shucking,
words, oysters plump with life. On Mooney Creek
the men stalk the tides for corruption.

They spend nights in tin shacks
that open at dawn onto our great brown river.
On the right tide they ride out

into the light in their punts, battered slabs
of aluminium with hundred-horse Yamahas on the stern
hammering tightly away, padded by hi-tech—

sucking mud into the cooling systems,
the motors leave a jet of hot piss in their wakes.
These power-heads indicate

the quality of the morning's hum.
The new boys don't wake from dreams
where clinkers crack, where mud sucks them under,

their grandfather's hands fumbling
accurately, loosening the knots. Back
at the bunker the hessian sacks are packed ready

and the shells grow into sliding white foothills.
A freezing mist clenches your fingers,
the brown stream now cold as fire:

plunge in and wash away last night's grog,
in the middle morning, stinging and wanting
the week to fold away until payday.

On the bank, spur-winged plovers stroll in pairs,
their beak-wattle chipped by frost,
each day blinking at the crack of sun.

Stalking for corruption? Signs.
Blue algae drifts through your brother's dream
of Gold Coasts, golf courses. The first settlement.

DRUM OF FIRE

Out the back my father's burning off—
drums of scrap, the lead casing
dripping from the copper wire,
toxic black smoke billowing into the air
each weekend, the lead trickling
down, molten rivulets spitting fire,
becoming deformed ingots. His
fuming shadow looming over
neat rows of vegetables.
In dreams I went back to school at night,
cutting through the alphabet,
torching examination papers, drunk
on fumes of kerosene, my fingers
marking strokes. At morning
assembly we sang the national anthem flat
with deadpan faces—I blew
into a flute for a whole term but wept
each night over my arithmetic
homework—then down to the Police Boys
boxing with the bigger kids until my
eyebrow bled too much. In the park
I flew with rainbow lorikeets
and hung upside down in the branches

of flowering coral trees. I sucked
nectar with them and stole their feathers;
prowled back lanes with a pair
of parrot's claws dried into spiky stars
in my pockets. Back home I'd stare
into my father's drum of flames—
conjuring images of the new Ford Thunderbirds
that came purring through our suburb,
and found no meaning in my father's fire
as he stashed another ton of scrap copper wire.

THE STONE CURLEW

I am writing this inside the head
of a bush stone curlew,
we have been travelling for days

moving over the earth
flying when necessary.
I am not the bird itself, only its passenger

looking through its eyes.
The world rocks slightly as we move
over the stubble grass of the dunes,

at night shooting stars draw lines
across the velvet dark
as I hang in a sling of light

between the bird's nocturnal eyes.
The heavens make sense, seeing this way
makes me want to believe

words have meanings,
that Australia is no longer a wound
in the side of the earth.

I think of the white settlers
who compared the curlew's song
to the cries of women being strangled,

and remember the poets who wrote
anthropomorphically as I sing softly
from the jelly of the stone curlew's brain.

ARCTIC JAEGER

This bird comes between the light
and your reading, hang-glides
in a corner of your eye, a pirate

with a feather in its cap—a sly con
riding the breath of your best line;
flying straight out of Olson's delirium tremens

hangs around with dead fish
under its wing; heavier than a night heron
like a loose-winged falcon:

take its shape to mean blood sport
on our terms. Lines drawn from the breath,
one flash of meaning following

another, a bad draft in its claw
a quote from Cohen's *The Future*
in its bill—this bird cuts out descriptions,

its flight over bleak oceans
tells no story, its white plumage a flying page
written in a language not endangered.

THE SOUTHERN SKUA

The skua flew into our heads in 1968—
a new kind of poetry, a scavenging predator
frequently attacking humans,
flying through the streets of seaside towns,
foraging with seagulls. This bird
has few predators. One was found
in Tasmania, its beak embedded in the skull
of a spotted quoll, dragged
into a clearing by devils. They form clubs
and proclaim their territory
by various displays and loud aggressive calls;
they are agile metaphysicians,
sweeping along lines of projective verse,
echoing each other's songs.
Although the skua breeds on Black Mountain
it is migratory and dispersive, its call
a series of low quacks and thin whinnying squeals.
They are omnivorous and critical creatures;
animal liberationists never mention
the habits of skua. If you read skua poetry, beware:
one could fly out from the page
and change the expression on your face.

SWIMMING OUT WITH EMMYLOU HARRIS

A long curved horizon, the hazel-coloured
tide and Lion Island
going by. A CD player skips
on the line *A quarter moon*

in a ten cent town, on the swell
our wake shatters the reflection
of the real moon. We cut
through the sound of swimming,

the meaningless joy of living,
the random punishment of birth.
The song says, we all live up to what
we get—out here you believe

whoever writes the script.
Yesterday is reflected back by the moon;
mothers wash the sickly
smell from a dozen ruined shirts

every Saturday afternoon. Wives
turn their heads. There's an old grey
stingray spread-eagled across
the front of the chicken run,

three crows hop around it, the breeze
ruffling their satin collars.
They plunge their black beaks
into the lukewarm flesh. Emmylou,

your sweet holy music drifts
through the new curtains,
your song folds itself around the shack
filling the backyard, flowing through

our days, out on the back veranda
where Old Dutch sits slumped two days
into his latest coma. Sweet Lord,
sweet poison, sweet, sweet music.

CROWS IN AFTERNOON LIGHT

How close can a human get to a crow,
how much do we know about them?
It's good to know we'll never read their brains,
never know what it means to be a crow.

All those crow poems are about poets—
none of them get inside the crow's head,
preen or rustle, let alone fly on crow wings.

No one knows what it is to sing crow song.

Five crows hop and stand around
the fish I have left for them on the wharf.
If I move their eyes follow me. I stand still
and they pick up a fish, test its weight,

then ruffle their feathery manes and shine.

These black bird shapes outlined by light,
behind them the river flowing out, the light
changing—soon it will be night

and they will be gone. Before that
I praise crows.

MEANING

A black summer night, no moon, the thick air
drenched with honeysuckle and swamp gum.

   In a pool of yellow torchlight
on a knife blade, the brand name
                        Hickey Miffle—
I give in to meaninglessness, look up
try to read smudges of ink
                        a live squid squirts
across the seats—now the smell of the river hones
an edge inside my brain,
      the night sky, Mallarmé's first drafts.

Who can I talk to now that you have left
the land of the living? The sound of more words.

The moon rolls out from the side of a mountain
and I decide to earn the rent;

      the net pours into a thick chop,
a line of green fire running before the moon's light—

Does four-inch mesh have anything to say tonight?

The mulloway might think so if they could—
Ah, Wordsworth, why were you so human?

On Friday nights I fork out comfort,
but tonight I work with holes, with absence.

I feed out a half-mile of mesh pulling the oars;
this comes once a life, a song without words
a human spider spinning a death web

across the bay. Alcohol, my friend my dark perversion,
here's to your damage:
who do you think you are?

My mother the belly dancer, my father Silence,
my house that repeats itself wherever I go.

THE NIGHT HERON

Midnight, my mind's full of ink tonight,
I'm drawing up some endings to make
a few last marks. Life's complete.
You're just part of the mix,
a pain cocktail, a dash of white spirit,
some pulvules of dextropropoxyphene
swallowed with black label
apple juice, as I cut and paste my past.

Life is sweet. Out there the night,
the stars in technicolour, a half-moon—
two half-moons, the black branches
of a mangrove tree. Jasmine's
heavy in the hot air, I feel alright
even here suspended in a humid room
with another summer to get through.
I write down words, they all seem fake,

so I crack them open. A night
writing letters to the future and the past—
if you could look into the present
you might see this pudgy figure at the desk
throwing back double shots of gin,

fumbling for cigarettes and a light
writing the word 'political' in a black
thin calligraphy. Wearing a pair of digital

blinkers set on zero. Outside the night
heron swings in from the heavens
and cuts through the aluminium light—
see its cream underwings, the grey breast,
the tan overcoat, watch it hit the pocket
of hot air, listen as it wheels on silence,
glides into the black calm above the swamp
and lands collecting in the creek.

TROPIC BIRD

Lord Howe Island

Wakes from nimbus cut to streaks
by the clipped volcanic peaks
mingle with an orange sky, the colour
of parrot-fish gut. Monsoon

time, nothing's quite right,
people drink or sleep or drift about.
On my deckchair's arm a tumbler
of gin has sucked in a dragonfly.

I drink myself sober as they say.
All that happens is my past
oozes through its pack of black jokes
and disasters. During *Under the Volcano*

I sucked bourbon through a straw
from a milkshake carton, at 4 a.m.
eating handfuls of ice cream,
I tried to sooth a hangover that went on

for a decade. I watched three
Siamese cats and as many marriages
sink with the fish. Always fish.
Tight water in black pools, moonlight

etching outlines of game-fishing boats
onto my brain—moored in slots,
fat with money yet taut, their
trimmings set to kill. I worked them,

sharpened hooks for high rollers,
sewing my special rigs—
bridles for bonito, live bait that
trailed the barbed viridian in our wake.

On the arm of my bamboo chair the glass
of gin is blossoming. The sky opens
and in sails, on black-edged wings,
a white, gracefully inhuman, tropic bird.

WINDY DROP DOWN CREEK

It was a blustering winter. I saw his name
in headlines, flapping outside a shop
next to the chemist. Death turns up
and life goes on incredibly, what can

you feel if the day turns to stone?
On the river the bowerbirds
dart through the mangroves in little troops,
the females trailing the colour

of their olive backs in streaks,
painting the air with olive-ribbons.
Whirring bowerbird light in quick curves
around their bowers flecked with

the blue tokens of their sex, the bits
of jagged indigo, the pegs of ultramarine,
spikes in cobalt and the dilatory
lapis lazuli of a male's eye

a pure blue deeper than cold blood
in a blocked vein. I remembered heroin's
white abyss and couldn't speak,
so turned with my little packet

from the chemist, walking out whistling
into the asphalt square of the car park.
Then I drove right around the block
to the grog shop: o vodka simplify the world.

While down in Calabash Creek the birds
whirred above their bowers trailing silky
olive ribbons, pushing time back and forth
uncovering and covering and calling up blue light.

AFTER BRETT WHITELEY

We're on this looping road, it's narrow
and the car's fast and expensive,
too fast considering we've downed a few.
There's a woman singing Bob Dylan well,

too well as the line about what you want
cuts through the climate control
mixing the smell of jonquils with hot
bodies. Things are looking dangerous.

Then suddenly the waters are before us,
the surface a black raw silk all ironed out
and drifting through a fishy light.
We are still in the car and quibbling

as a wild duck makes an evanescent wake
across the phosphorous tide. The woman turns
to Brett and says: is this decadence? No man,
he mutters, just reflected glory up shit creek.

CREON'S DREAM

The old hull's spine shoots out of the mudflat,
a black crooked finger pointing back to the house.
On the dead low the smell of the mangroves.

The river seeps through the window, the books
are opened out on the desk. When the first breeze
hits the curtain the cats scatter.

It could be dawn for all I know, concentration
wanders through Creon's words to Antigone
Go to the dead and love them—okay so they live as

long as I do—what else can I make of it?
The bright feathers from a crimson rosella lie
in clumps on the floor with a pair of broken wings.

In the dark I try to write and remember the zoo
I played in as a child. There was a balding sedated lion
and a wedge-tailed eagle hunched on a dead

tree in a cage; they threw it dead rabbits
in 1953. The whooping cranes sidestepped
the concrete ponds and whooped all night.

The blue heron flaps across the river in my head,
poddy mullet hanging from its tight beak.
Ah, dead fish, the old black crow, the sick pelican.

I pad the room, out there mangroves are pumping up
the putrid air, life goes on. At the zoo they
still throw the animals dead meat, the big cats

are bred in labs where they lock the albino
freaks away. I pace the kitchen: where are the books,
who reads the poems? I take a drink, ribbonfish

swim across my pages, I shake my head but they swim on—
in low flocks, chromium ribbons, they fly under
the river herding up the poddy mullet,

rippling the surface, as the tawny frogmouth knows.
The books have gone, the spoonbills wade in
with whitebait skipping ahead of them,

channel-billed cuckoos come swooping after the crows,
flying low over the water, calling their mates,
dipping their hooked beaks into the moving chrome.

I sleep in broken snatches and dream nothing.
Mosquitoes suck at my cheeks and empty bottles
clutter the verandah, the books are in darkness

but the sandy whimbrels finger the pages, words
dissolve, waves of the dead arrive in dreams.
Out there the black finger points to the mouth

of the river, where the dead are heading, they
move over the window glass. The extinct fins move
the fingers of my grandfather, mending nets,

the dead friends sing from invisible books. The heron
picks the bloodshot eyes from my father's terrible
work in the kilns and the darkness is complete.

THE WHITE ABYSS

After a life, the next decade
is a concept I must comprehend—
Time, wrote Augustine, is some kind of trick.

He asked his God to forgive him
for thinking along these lines,
it had to be done.

What happens next? Outside
Hell smoulders as usual,
inside, electricity and words.

Everything exists to end in the book.

I live in Mallarmé's head for days
nothing happens and this
is paradise, thoughts
unfold instead of flowers, abstract and warm.

I have not experienced a grief
as devastating as the black abyss
the death of Anatole left—
this is a corner of the head I prefer
not to revisit

when I go back the intensity
of the experience of loss leaves me empty.

This is death then, a blank
where no thought flowers, a pit of black
tideless water, where no fish kill.

Here you realize you can live through anything,
stripped, without a head, your soul
shown up for the joke souls are.

Then you begin to understand Augustine.

THE GATHERING LIGHT

Morning shines on the cowling of the Yamaha
locked onto the stern of the boat,
spears of light shoot away
from the gun-metal grey enamel.
Now I wait for God to show
instead of calling him a liar.

I've just killed a mulloway—
it's eighty-five pounds, twenty years old—
the huge mauve-silver body trembles in the hull.

Time whistles around us, an invisible
flood tide that I let go
while I take in what I have done.
It wasn't a fight, I was drawn to this moment.
The physical world drains away
into a golden calm.

The sun is a hole in the sky, a porthole—
you can see turbulence out there,
the old wheeling colours and their dark forces—
but here on the surface of the river

where I cradle the great fish in my arms
and smell its pungent death, a peace
I've never known before—a luminous absence
of time, pain, sex, thought, of everything
but the light.

ON NOT SEEING PAUL CÉZANNE

I think of the waste, the long
years of not believing the
tongue pretending

in the midst of words
to speak, to keep walking
that bend in the road

I cursed myself for not having spoken

The blank sheets of air could have added

Words smudged out and revised with a colour

stroked instead of butting
coming to the shape by layers, stumbling
in from the corners and rubbing out the hard light

The countless fish flapping on boards
Have they just disappeared?
There's no way

back to the water to catch
again that possible
colour

Outside the window in the black night
mosquitoes gather under floodlights on the pontoon
until the empty westerly blows

Everything that matters comes together
slowly, the hard way, with the immense and tiny details,
all the infinite touches, put down onto nothing—

each time we touch
it begins again, love quick brushstrokes
building up the undergrowth from the air into what holds

ÉVENTAIL: FOR MERY IN PARIS

Writing this in sepia ink on a Japanese fan,
pain slants my calligraphy
this way, sex just under the cap of my skull.

Dreams taunt your existence
as you swish by in raw silk
until the words I use lose meaning

and my best lines twang like limp
old lace. This metaphor thick with blood
trembles as my mind approaches the blank

folds in the rice paper, writing
on your arms, this scrawl scrolling
through you, each letter a link in the chain

between my head and the bed, a text
of splintering syllables in which
time comes apart, pricking your skin—

the joke's our meaning, gnarled
with the word-knots coming undone
where your breast shines with the sepia

ink and the sheets blot out thinking.
Smudged with love, your bum's a haze
of lavender oil as I rub this in.

THE YELLOW BITTERN

At Uladulla
a bittern puffs out its neck feathers,
head between wings—

slits of eyes tight in the wind
flinging sand, hammering grains of stone
against it.

Our bird of words falls apart—
its wings without vowels,
its head empty of tough money.

O bittern, come off it, talk to us
about when we were young: that first
kiss hissing as she bit my tongue.

THE COWBIRD

This is not poetry—this bird's turkey-head
has a craw that produces crap—its chicks,
    feeding, get covered in a stench
    you could compare

to the breath of an alcoholic cane toad
that's feasted on a bucket of rancid pork.
    The descriptive drift
    throws up this internationalist:

the hoatzin (pronounced *what-seen*),
lives on the banks of the Orinoco River
    flowing through the central
    plains of Venezuela.

Young hoatzins dive-bomb the surface
from their nests overhead, swim
    underwater then pull themselves
    back up into the trees

with their clawed wingtips.
The idea of these creatures has been known
    to drive scientific investigators
    crazy: infesting the imaginations

of phytochemists from within,
they create themselves from the dark
    whims of their hosts, parachuting
    in through their eyes.

Good students have fried their brains
contemplating the mating habits
    of the cowbird—they are, however, pure
    joy to confessional poets,

who weave them in as tropes as they write poems
concerning their wedding night, in which they
    consummate their bliss oozing
    the milk of *what-seens.*

THE HUDSONIAN GODWIT

Although it breeds in Hudson Bay,
it winters in South America.
However, a lone vagrant godwit
was found at Kooragang Island
in New South Wales before
the Christmas of 1982—word
spread quickly and many observers
travelled to Newcastle to see it.
They are still searching. This
Australian godwit's call—*toy, toy, toy*—
was recorded and this recording
has been compared to the work
of Phil Spector. Its markings are
complex and beautiful, with
prominent white supercilium,
dorsum deep grey with each feather
fringed white, its underparts mainly
soot-grey. It is a bird for objectivists.
It wades through the shallows,
its bill making rapid stitching motions
as it sews together its own wake.
The godwit's cryptic markings
make it a perfect object for the similes
of Australia's 'greatest imagist'—
but don't look, you won't find it.

LETTER TO ROBERT CREELEY

I've heard the system's closing down. It's good
reading in books, old friend, your words about
what a friend is, if you have one. These
days I often think of Zukofsky
just throwing in the word
'objectivist' and how it works
as well as any label could. These
days we're just words away
from death and I think
I've finally learnt to listen (your love
songs seem wise now that the years
have steadied my head) as you turn hurt
without sentiment to gain. I thought
of your clear humour when my father
was dying of cancer. I asked about the pain
and he spun me a line: 'it feels like a big
mud crab having a go at my spine.'

CORNFLOWERS

There are no cornflowers here—
the sunlight slants through
the glass, the harbour
glitters, ruffled by a light
westerly. The jacaranda tree
is in flower and almost
comes through the open
window. Honeysuckle
perfume, channel-billed
cuckoos, and huge fruit bats
come with night—in the darkness
neon signs throwing red and blue
reflections across the surface
of the tide. Sydney Harbour Bridge
is a dark arch with lights blooming.
I pick up the empty vase and place it
on the table, knowing that when you
enter the room, it will be filled
with the missing flowers.

EURYDICE IN SYDNEY

What was he thinking while I was gone?
Was his mind still doing time in his head,
dancing in abstract darkness?

Pain comes and goes. I notice things
I hadn't before: the city ibis stitching its voice
to the wind between car park and George Street.

I think of going shopping with him.
Bogong moths in a shaft of sunlight
flutter beneath the blue trees

of a shadowy Hyde Park. Does
Sydney Harbour still exist? Depends
on how his voice murmurs

late into night as he drinks, rustling
still with that old ardour, trailing ribbons
of smoke and blood.

REACHING LIGHT

for Bracha L. Ettinger

Where was it we left from?
We say the journey's up, but maybe

memory sinks deeper.
Our journey so far

has been quiet, the only
incident being that rock dislodged

as he spun around on his heel.
What was that stuff—brimstone?

The first slice of sunlight glanced off
a slab of dark marble that turned to glow.

His back moved ahead of me—
his curls, shoulders,

that neck. What new bone was he inventing
in his shuffling head, what chance

that a doorway would appear and then a house?
The dark supported me, comfortably

behind me, a cradle woven from
demon hair. As I rose

and climbed toward day, his turning head,
those eyes—strips of memory,

silver tides, moons rising over the
rim of the world—

brought back the day we were married,
standing in fine rain, then escaping from family,

sex by a rolling surf in a high wind, velvet
heavens and the stars omens:

calendars, clocks, zodiacs—
straight, bent signs.

3

A BEND IN THE EUPHRATES

In a dream on a sheet of paper I saw
a pencil drawing of lovers: they seemed perfect,
Adam and Eve possibly. Stepping into reality,
I read lines of a poem on a piece
of crumpled rag I kept trying to smooth—Egyptian
linen, so fine it puzzled to imagine such a delicate
loom. In a flash I saw two dirty-breasted ibis
and heard their heads swish: black bills
swiped the cloudy stream, and in the rushes
I heard needles stitching, weaving features
into the landscape, clacking as they shaped
an orange tree, then switched a beat to invent
blue-black feathers for crows, the pointed
wedges of their beaks. A fox rustles
through wild lantana as I step through into
the garden and, becoming part of the weave,
notice the tide turn, its weight eroding mudbanks,
bringing filth in from the ocean. A raft of flotsam
breaks away, a duckling perched on the thicket
of its hump. I use the murky river for my ink,
draw bearings on the piece of cloth, sketch
a pair of cattle egrets bullying teal into flight.
The map's folded away. I travel by heart now,

old lessons are useless. I shelter from bad weather
in the oyster farmer's shack. The moon falls in a
column of light, igniting a glowing epicycle
—this pale spot on my writing table,
these fragments of regret.

THE GREENSHANK

Miklós Radnóti, marched from forced labour
in Yugoslavia back into Hungary, came to rest
near a bend in the Rábca, at what his translator
describes as 'a strange lonely place' where

the tributary joins 'the great river', a marshland
watched over by willows and 'high circling birds'.
Condors perhaps—they appear in the notes and
poems he was writing—under a foamy sky.

Huddled in a trench with the body of a friend
who'd been shot in the neck, he wrote with a pencil
stub in his notebook: *patience flowers into death*.
His wife's face bloomed in his head.

Thinking of the petals of crushed flowers
floating in a wake of perfume, he wrote to caress her
neck. The fascists' bullets wiped out his patience.
His written petals survive.

Today, we listen to the news of war
here in a river sanctuary my wife's unbending
will has created—horizontal slats of cedar, verticals
of glass—a Mondrian chapel of light.

This afternoon just before dark the first
greenshank arrived from the Hebrides.
Ignorant of human borders, its migration
technology is simple: feathers

and fish-fuel, cryptic colour and homing
instinct. This elegant wader landed on a mooring,
got ruffled in the westerly, then took off again,
an acrobatic twister, and levelled down

onto a mudflat—a lone figure that dashed across
the shore, stood on one leg, then, conducting
its song with its bill, came forward
in a high-stepping dance.

THE FLOATING HEAD

I turned off electricity, pulled telephone cords
out of the wall, saw stars in glass through cedar slats.
I wrapped a scarf around my headache
and looked inside—

an ebbing memory leaving with the tide.
My boat's motor roared and I hurtled across
the river into blazing cold night
then circled back.

Crouched in a corner of the house,
my cat borrows my voice—I talk
to him through the night. The heater
clicks, its pilot light blinks. I scribble

a few lines, pass my fishing rod off
as a lyre. Who needs this bitter tune?
Its distorted chords lull me into numbness.
I bend it over double and pluck.

EURYDICE AND THE MUDLARK

Sunlight fades the coloured spine
of *What Bird Is That?* The shadow

of your hand marks my face:
wings and the tips of fingers,

coiled hands in the tiny egg
or sac of living tissue,

dredge up a likeness beyond
appearance. Morning unfurls,

I wake and shave. In the mirror
the reflection of a mudlark's tail-fan

echoes the silence of glass.
We hover all day on the surface

of the stream, above a soft bottom,
until moonlight falls again

onto stark white bedsheets.
The shadow your hand casts

resembles the mudlark, opening
its wings, calling and rocking,

perched in the pages
of my book.

EURYDICE AGAPE

A preacher came to Calabash Creek
in an expensive four-wheel drive.
He set up in the little park
with his team of technicians.
Bose speakers hung from the gum trees.
The kookaburras started laughing
just before dark.

An oyster farmer's punt, full of
drunks from the Workers Club,
took off from the mudflats and roared
into the night. They called us a bunch
of cunts. Before long the children
from the point were speaking
in tongues. The singing

was fabulous—a woman sang
the Statesboro Blues—and there
was talk of miracles. Then the
preacher spoke of Hell. Suddenly
my arms were full, you started
sobbing, my face was wet with tears.
You were back in paradise.

THINKING OF EURYDICE AT MIDNIGHT

My Siamese cat's left a brown
snake, its back broken, on my desk.
The underground throbs outside my window.
The black highway of the river's crinkled by a light
westerly blowing down. I want to give praise
to the coming winter, but problems
of belief flare and buckle under
the lumpy syntax. The unelected
President's on the radio again,
laying waste to the world.

Faith—that old lie. I drag up
impossible meanings and double divisions
of love and betrayal, light and dark.
Where on earth am I after all these years?
A possum eats crusts on the verandah,
standing up on its hind legs.
My weakness can't be measured.
My head contains thousands of images—
slimy mackerel splashing about in the murk.
My failures slip through fingers pointed
at the best night of my life. This one.

The cold mist falls, my head floats in a stream
of thinking. Eurydice. Did I fumble? Maybe
I was meant to be the moon's reflection
and sing darkness like the nightjar. Why
wouldn't I infest this place, where the
sun shines on settlers and their heirs
and these heirlooms I weave
from their blond silk?

THE VOYAGE

We looked up at Scorpio's tail of stars
curved across light years of night.
We anchored and made love in the dark,

embraced in the cold before dawn and spoke
of Novalis who praised nocturnal light.
Although my thoughts were dark,

you spoke of those who spoke of light
as they moved through the night:
old saints and fishermen following stars.

The river flowed towards morning
until Scorpio grew pale, fading with dawn,
and darkness sailed into light.

RAINBOW BEE-EATERS

Wings fuelled
by the knowledge of bees

turning on axles of air
each crescent beak

an orange-coloured talisman
Once snowy-headed elders

gathered honey bags
in turpentine forests

feathery blurs eating bees
hovering miracles

alongside ancient cliffs
flashed brightly

Your film exposed to them
transparencies

to stay love by catching day
light on pages

the translucent calligraphy
of wings

THE RUFF

It's difficult to describe the ruff.
This bird's a live metaphor, puffing
its plumage into simile. A rough
attempt at meaning: though a
waterbird, it dances onshore.

Its colours? Sepia, cream, and
specks of red. These tones bleed well
for watercolourists, but a cock ruff
in display looks top-heavy, often
toppling over into absurdity or worse.

Ruff 's a word from the sixteenth century:
feathers goffered into ornaments
for sex. Ritual is human. These cock
birds blow up by instinct, strutting
as if to get across how inhuman

they are, how utterly bird. They
dance in lines of ruff music; some
have suggested that a feather's cadence,
once heard, conducts this dance—
a puffed pose, its head hidden by dark

cowling and the eyes blinded by display.
The ruff's ways delight us if we have
a sense of humour or a dash of
madness: the way of the ruff
is for folk who take themselves

seriously, for this bird's habits
contradict words, art, and human
silence. A ruff occurs at the fringes
of things, in the gap between it
and words. Ruff.

NOT A PENNY SONNETS

for Gig Ryan

1

A book launch, plates of water biscuits.
'There's always the club sandwich,' you said.
But the corporate types didn't get it—they were
busy being freaks—so we spliced letters into words
as verbal tattoos, using anything we'd written,
digging our biros in. A girl drives by
in a low-slung Torana. Remember the suburbs,
those days of ordinary defeat? Using street directories
so out of date they didn't show the streets?
We had dreams of driving racing cars. These days
we can afford to trade quips at the Intercontinental,
go to funerals, throw out old affections. Drinking
beer and double gins, I'm talking
but nothing seems to grip.

2

I've written my response before you speak:
'Well, fiddle-de-dee,' we said to the police,
walking onto the illuminated page,
being freaks, digging our biros in. We honed
our beaks on cuttlefish bones from your baptismal
swim, stringing along the corporate types, filling
shot glasses to the brim in our separate skins.
Cracks? Take a bite and your teeth might ache
with old affections and lost destinations.
We sharpened the edge for decades, drinking hard,
looking for something to blame. Remember smoking
ready-mades? You demanded things—impossible—
from me. I had nothing, not a penny to my name,
just references, chips, and lemonade.

3

We scoff at good luck from the Intercontinental,
flash Medicare cards before signing anything.
Our biros dig into *Gone with the Wind*, breathing
air-conditioned memories in separate skins—
goose pimples, anti-fashion, enemies, and friends.
Back on the street, we take in the city.
A Torana spins its wheels, skeins of brown smoke
clog the pavement—she's gone. But we're still
standing here, talking, destroying words.
The club sandwich? Well, fiddle-de-dee. We believe
nothing: the shredded trust, the corporate types—
just limping figures in dressed skin. The life
we mocked surrounds us—distracted,
but the tide keeps coming in.

THE PEACH-FACED
FINCHES OF MADAGASCAR

I cart home sugarbags of coke from the gasworks.
My hands mark the cream-painted icebox. My father
throws spuds on the fire, sending sparks up the flue.

On the hill outside, trucks growl and strip their gears.
I imagine the peach-faced finches of Madagascar.
After tea, Dad slumps in his chair, tall brown bottles

standing empty on the table. At school each day I fail
my tests. My mother's face hardens when I try to speak.
She irons starch into my sister, from her straight black

hair to her school uniform's box pleats. In the back yard,
cuckoo chicks squawk from a magpie's nest. The hedge
man's finished clipping hedges along our street.

My brothers bob down to do their homework, into
the learning stream, heading for their lives,
biting the heads off words.

THE DOLLARBIRD

As the family listened to the reading
of the will, dollarbirds were landing,
summer migrants thudding into soft
magnolia trees in bloom. It seems
I'll be able to free this captive life
of my mind, let it fall from my eyes
like fish scales and just walk away—
now she'll be okay financially at least.
My conscience, the bully, keeps honing
these blunt threats daily. How much
freedom will she take, how many lozenges
of grief in brown paper bags? I'll scatter
rotten fruit on the terrace and every flying
insect on the northern peninsula will loop
and scuttle in droves for the feast. Dollarbirds
will hawk for them in the air. Translucent,
she glides through my thoughts reading
The Divine Comedy in the compartment
I've filed her in. Bad? Sure, but there's more
housework to be done in my head today.
Pawpaws rot efficiently—they attract pests
from miles away, hovering and crawling.
As she listens, her cheeks glow, her thoughts

swerve as elegantly as dollarbirds gathering
the words to strike. There's a cavil, a hiccup
and a shudder down her spine. Thirty years
of gibberish, resentments drenched in perfume,
years of love and an inkling she could be wrong.
Can I siphon off the fertilizing fantasy and let
passion wither like old skin? Unpleasant
metaphors vanish, migrate back to where
those green-feathered beakies come from:
a dollarbird tumbles as it flies above
magnolia trees in bloom.

THE GOLDFINCHES OF BAGHDAD

These finches are kept in gold cages
or boxes covered in wire mesh;
they are used by falcon trainers as lures,
and rich patriarchs choose these living ornaments
to sing to them on their deathbeds. Their song is pure
and melodious. A goldfinch with a slashed throat
was the subject of a masterpiece painted in the
sixteenth century on the back of a highly
polished mother-of-pearl shell—it burns
tonight in Baghdad, along with the living,
caged birds. Flesh and feathers, hands
and wings. Sirens wail, but the tongues
of poets and the beaks of goldfinches burn.
Those who cannot speak burn along with the
articulate—creatures oblivious to prayer burn
along with those who lament to their god.
Falcons on their silver chains, the children
of the falcon trainer, smother in the smoke
of burning feathers and human flesh.
We sing or die, singing death
as our songs feed the flames.

FISHING IN A
LANDSCAPE FOR LOVE

This is swampland, its mountains
worn down by the wings of kingfishers
flying back to their nests. Crows
are black feathers

saving me from morning.
I talk to them as if we're friends,
they look at me sideways.
When I offer them fish they eat it.

Swamp harriers whistle as they do
slow circles through the azure—
let's talk about the azure.
Descriptions of place

can't imitate the legs of prawns
moving gently in the tide
from which the azure takes on meaning.
I put them into a mosquito-wire cage

and lower them from the jetty,
they jump from their sleep
on the dark of the moon.
Bait is all that matters here—

love's worn down into sound
and is contained in what I say,
these dead words feeding on live ones,
these ideas thrown to the crows—

they don't come back.
Love needs live bait,
it doesn't behave
like a scavenger.

THE FIRST CHANCE WAS THE LAST

Down sandstone steps to the jetty—always
the same water, lights scattered across tide.
Remember, we say, the first time.
Our eyes locked into endless permission,

this dark gift. Why can't I let go
and be the man in your life—not the one who writes
your name on the dedication page; whatever
the name, you know who I write for,

you know how private, how utterly selfish
these musings are. This is your image,
crafted in the long hours away. The house
rocks, money comes and goes, fish

jump against tide. The children grow
and go out into the world. The bleak eye
turns, my tongue speaks with ease—a rudder
steering the stream of words into their

daily meanings. I cried out when you weren't
here, I smashed my fist against stone. Art was stone.
A red glow cracked the kitchen window. I carved
the roast and served it to the cats.

Signposts point the way. Bitter laughter stings,
my black heart beats. This way to the shops
and gallery in the ordinary day. Clap your
hands against my ears, turn off the lights—

you stay. Is it *always* you? Shapes change,
music becomes a pool of melancholy seawater
distilled in sun, slapping rock, then a seagull's eye
reflecting a shoal of whitebait alive with death.

Love makes an art that walks in a son
and moves a daughter. We move
through time and sing in the light:
the first chance was the last.

ELEGY FROM BALMORAL BEACH

for Arkie Deya Whiteley

A beach. Small waves and a shark net.
Moonlight on a fig tree, the bay a black mirror.

Music coming from a house, an exquisite guitar.
Tonight, there's nothing more bitter.

Resonating chords float above the school yard,
night birds beat the humid air. The ebb tide

exposes the moon's haul: squabbling seagulls
slicing open the body of a drowned rat.

A light flickers, a newspaper floats. Doc Watson's
playing sounds like a waterfall, almost gentle.

Tonight the harbour's incandescent.
You arrive in an empty boat.

PRAISE AND ITS SHADOW

Standing on this rocky shore
at the end of the point, sun's
hitting sandstone escarpments as it sinks,
colouring everything red—
I watch the felty black surface
of the river carrying pelicans
downstream to the mouth.
I could easily disappear into
this landscape, become
a fisherman again and work
the tide through the moon's cycles
and its darks, pierced with stars—
a local Novalis, courting
the night itself—my nets always
coming in without a catch,
at dawn each new day my head full
of emptiness, nothing there
but love for the long, echoing darkness.

DEATH OF A CAT

Siamese seal-pointer, ghost cat.
My familiar and killer,
sleeper under covers.
A true carnivore
devoured hundreds of pilchards,
maybe thousands,
and many baby brown snakes.

That pair of kingfisher bodies.
First the pale female,
jumped and tortured.
Then the male
who returned to help his mate
and met death by tooth and claw.

Roller of lizards and skinks,
blue-eyed and sleek.

Bully-boy with a foul tongue,
most articulate at night.
Shiny, cream-furred cuddler,
brown-eared stalker.
Attention seeker and birdwatcher.
My wife's tormentor.

The one who ate a dozen
live garfish whole,
stolen from the bait-tank.
Taut-bodied, razor-footed climber
with sprung rhythm.
Stuck among branches yowling.

Ripping the chairs apart,
while purring for praise.
A 'legend' according to my son,
to my wife, a demented prowling beast.

My darling and terrible
King Tut, who prowled here
for eighteen years before The Mower
cut out his kidneys.

THE WHITEBAIT

The first winter frost
burns delicate leaves
of basil in terracotta pots,

coats the kangaroo-paw
ferns; white fur collars
on crimson buds.

The hardy starlings
flit about, pecking dirt;
singing, click, click.

I read the morning news
and then think of
the unblinking eyes

of silver gulls—
their beaks slash at
whitebait still kicking

in plastic boxes on the wharf
of the Fisherman's Co-op.

In our garden, a patch
of sunlight moves across
the grass, eating the crystals of ice.

JOSEPH CORNELL'S TOOLS

Joseph Cornell used these sturdy tools
and instruments to create boxes,
time machines. Constructions
made from bits and pieces,
three-dimensional frames containing
fans, lace, feathers—other
once-ephemeral objects, including
a torn fragment of photography,
an image of Mallarmé's
hands—one contains an illustration
of a hummingbird—it seems
to hover in the space between
the glass and the backing of the box.
In another, an etching
of a great horned owl—like the bird
I watched one night,
perched on a light-post in Boulder,
Colorado: it swoops from
memory, filling my study with silent
flight as I recall another
visitation. This afternoon,
returning from the post office
I drove ahead of an approaching storm,

trees shook and a black cockatoo
flew out of them, it sailed on
just ahead of my car for almost a minute,
a long time given the situation—
stroking the air before the windscreen,
following the road, so close
I could see details of its plumage,
two red patches across the tail feathers.
Something other than beautiful, fleeting.

LOOKING INTO A
BOWERBIRD'S EYE

Untamable, fluttering, a feathery
cold pulsing in my hands—
a mature male bowerbird.
House-glow, the night outside,
here the kitchen light reflects
electric splinters, uncountable
shards clustered in a blue eye.
Everything flares to a beak
pecking at fingers, claws
raking the palm of my hand,
alembic depths of blue eye-tissue.
He was trapped in a cupboard at 3 a.m.:
the cat's voice woke the house.
Fingers flecked with specks
of blood now, the eye
a fiery well of indigo cells, cobalt,
ultramarine, cerulean blues.
A pale moon slips through
tree branches outside—
the windowpane frames its quarter,
then a squall of refracted
light in eyes that a human

cannot read—opaque, steadfast.
Light-sensitive molecules, intricate
lenses, a blue cone of tissue.
Outside, bracing night air, the stars
clustered in the Milky Way—
my hands, opening, flicked by wings.

LISTENING TO CUCKOOS

Two unchanging notes; to us, words—always those high
elongated notes. Red-eyed koels with feathered earmuffs,

downward-ending notes that pour through a falling of night
coming over the distances, words that don't change.

The two notes remain, a split phrase, two words
meaning, not exactly a self—not quite, the first day of spring.

The moment of utterance, candour becomes
the piercing, whistled syllables. Penetrating the dark green

of twilight, the storm birds call, two notes, two words,
and cackle in the broken-egged dawn, in the echoing light.

SUMMER

after Georg Trakl

A pallid cuckoo calls in a loop
more insistently as afternoon fades.

In garden beds humid air
clings to the stalks of poppies.

Mosquitoes rise from layers
of leaves under grapevines.

A blue shirt sticks to your back
as you climb the ladder.

Thunder rattles a fishing boat's
canopy in the dry dock.

The storm silences crickets
chirruping under the mangroves.

Turbulence has passed.
A candle lights our dark room.

Outside, calm, a starless night—
then the flame is extinguished,

pinched between a finger
and thumb. In the eaves, at nest,

swallows rustle. You believe
the swallows glow in the dark.

Light daubs our skin with shapes—
the crushed petals of red poppies.

GARDEN POEM

for Juno

Sunlight scatters wild bees across a blanket
of flowering lavender. The garden

grows, visibly, in one morning—
native grasses push up, tough and lovely

as your angel's trumpets. At midday
the weather, with bushfire breath, walks about

talking to itself. A paper wasp zooms
above smooth river pebbles. In the trees

possums lie flat on leafy branches to cool off,
the cats notice, then fall back to sleep.

This day has taken our lives to arrive.
Afternoon swings open, although

the mechanics of the sun require
the moon's white oil. Daylight fades to twilight

streaking bottlebrush flowers with shade;
a breeze clatters in the green bamboo and shakes

its lank hair. At dinnertime, the French doors present us
with a slice of night, shining clear—

a Naples-yellow moon outlines the ridges
of the mountains—all this, neatly laid out

on the dining room table
across patches of moonlight.

VIA NEGATIVA, THE DIVINE DARK

1. A POEM WITHOUT BIRDS

My Worthiness is all my Doubt —Emily Dickinson

This morning the tree-ferns woke and opened out
as sunlight dispersed a thick mist—
    morning in a memory incised

with old phrases, mouthing
words then uttering a sentence with an unfinished
    breath. Banana trees rustle,

a first breeze arrives, bringing the perfumes
of the ebb; watermarks down on the mudflats begin
    to disappear.

Morning turns its back on the sun;
gradually, night arrives. In the skylight,
stars appear through the smokescreen from a burn-off,
    brilliant pinholes.

Stars are clustered trees, hung in the night sky.

Whose body, whose eyes? Look
up into the heavens: the problem of suffering

expands forever—dust and light again,
maybe time, if it exists.

On the table a cicada, flecked with flour,
opening its dry cellophane wings.

The cat flies across polished space illuminated by the
kitchen's energy-saving light bulb,
a Philips 'Genie'.

Life like a dirty wind blowing straight
through a snowy head, cat eyes, tint of fur, a rustling.
Praise life   with broken words.

2. A PRELIMINARY SKETCH

What I see not, I better see —Emily Dickinson

An old shack by the river, deserted for years now,
haunted by mesh nets and anchor rope,

wild apple trees grow out the back.
A charcoal sketch of this scene unfurls before me

on a sheet of mist, I push aside tough vines of
morning glory and then walk on, into the drawing.

It's difficult to move in this landscape,
and I have forgotten the names of most flora and fauna.

Crosshatched charcoal enfolds me
and I become a part of the subject matter, my shape

drawn carefully, sharp and figurative.
However, precision no longer interests me:

my attention is focused by smudges, the forms
grown vague—just fifty years ago

a country of sandstone and gums, a second ago
ferns and hardship. The heavy tidal swings

roll corks and drown fish caught by their gills
in the smothering mesh. In the distance bushfire

writes its killer lines—orange loops, burning serifs
spill over the sandstone escarpments.

I fished these tides when I was young
and abstract—what rubbed off, what idea sunk home?

I rejected the lessons and feared my mother's God,
the Christ I couldn't believe in. The friends

in those days, the ones I loved, are now drawn
beside me in the margins. The kirk

we attended appears, the place where the minister
refused to tell me exactly what a soul might be—

although mine, come Judgment Day,
would be flung into Hell, along with the others

who weren't chosen. The Presbyterian soul
is not mysterious, rather it's something we were

lumped with. Now I rise from the sketch,
my face smeared with ink from years of sinning—

back on the river, my boat plows through fog.
I'm looking hard. What form, shape, or song

might represent a soul? What words, paint, or mud
resemble such an intangible glow?

A stain of mist hangs above a blackbutt,
brushed by the wings of a grey-headed flying fox.

NET MAKERS

They stitched their lives into my days,
Blues Point fishermen, with a smoke
stuck to their bottom lips, bodies bent

forward, inspecting a haul-net's wing
draped from a clothes line. Their hands
darting through mesh, holding bone

net needles, maybe a special half-needle
carved from tortoise shell. Their fingers,
browned by clusters of freckles

and tobacco tar, slippery with speed—
they wove everything they knew
into the mesh, along with the love they had,

or had lost, or maybe not needed.
During my school holidays I watched them
and came to love this craft

of mending, in our backyard by the harbour,
surrounded by copper tubs brimming
with tanning soup brewed from

bloodwood and wild-apple bark.
These men could cut the heart clean
from a fish with a swipe of a fillet knife

and fill buckets with gut flecked
with the iridescent backs of flies
as it fermented into liquid fertilizer.

I'd water my father's beds of vegetables,
rows of silverbeet, a fence of butterbeans.
In the last of the sun, I'd watch

our peacock spread its fan; the hose
sprayed water from a water tank, house high,
fed by gravity.

HEAVING THE ROPE

A ferry kisses the wharf—
engine rumble, shudder,
and prop-churn stir
the tide to white foam.
A deck hand makes a line
then heaves his rope,
lassos a bollard.
There's a golden codger
fishing for blackfish,
his long rod and float,
green weed for bait.
The local boys, wharf rats
who fish all hours.
A businessman in bright
pinstripes walks
the gangplank. Boys
at Manly, diving from
pylons for silver coins,
girls off to Luna Park
or to school on the other
shore. The ferry's
deckie ropes in the life
of the harbour—his
world framed by seagulls
and southerly busters—
when he heaves the rope.

CHOWDER BAY

The nights at Chowder Bay were illegible.
Out from the wharf, the bottom
dropped off into a deep valley.
Past squid and circling yellowtail,
ribbonfish hovered in the water column,
swimming vertically, like chrome-plated
seahorses. In the darkness
before dawn a blanket of mist
would float across the tide—
when the sun rose, it seemed a pale hole
in morning's roof. Our baits
became bleached and tough,
the wharf gradually disappeared in fog.
Cold air cramped our fingers.
Around 9 a.m. the white haze
lifted—then macaws from Taronga Zoo
flew in, flaring with reds
and blues. They'd pull green curtains
apart and take centre stage,
exotic escapees, then fly to our side
of the bay. We watched as their beaks
flashed in sun, red-tipped question marks
punctuating empty branches of jacaranda trees.

THE RIVER CAVES

We were keen young cubs, members
of Third Mosman Bay Sea Scouts,
twelve years old and full
of excitement, collecting donations
for the clubhouse charity.
On bob-a-job week we walked
up and down steep streets
around the harbour, mowing
lawns, raking leaves, taking
on any work we were offered.
A woman asked us to remove
a huge white carp from one
of her garden ponds:
dead for a week, its smell clung
to our uniforms all day—
she had a mansion with a
suburban jungle surrounding it.
One Saturday morning
we ended up at Luna Park,
wandered in, and came across
the River Caves—a ride
that carried us in brightly
painted boats through dark

tunnels to illuminated caverns.
By the time we entered
the second cave we were looking
for trouble. The next cave
was an artificial South Pole,
with ice and hundreds of penguins.
I jumped out first
and the others followed. Our boat
moved on so fast it left us
stranded. We heard the next one
coming, and, not to be caught,
I told my friends to 'freeze'—as if
we were models of cubs in a landscape,
the frozen Sea Scouts of the River Caves.

THE SHARK-NET
SEAHORSES OF BALMORAL

for Peter Kingston

The swimmers changed into their day clothes
and left the beach to the cleaner, a man
with a spike and rake. Night came and went.
The fishing boy walked onto the sand alone.
At dawn the sky beyond the Heads
flared into sheets of light, as if bombs were
exploding on some distant island. Thunder
was absent and silence wasn't reassuring.
He was in tune with details of the beach,
the calm above yellow sand—a bay with water

clear as white spirit—blue-ringed octopus,
sepia kelp with drifting sharkskin leaves.
Some mornings penguins would swim in and dive
for slender garfish, surface, then bob and shake
their turquoise heads. Below the scattering
school of gar, whiting cruised for worms.
The beach was the boy's world, on the ebb
he'd collect stranded starfish and throw them back:
first the locals with long spindle legs, then squat
comic stars, dark-red aliens from Manly.

He loved an underwater fence, a shark net,
hung from a steel cable strung across the bay
from the Island to its anchor embedded
in the wall of a concrete stormwater outlet.
He'd spit into his goggles and adjust a snorkel,
then float across an inverted world: stingrays were
birds of prey—the prawns, crabs, and lobsters,
insects of the eelgrass and the rocks.
The shark net was a hanging garden under the tide,
beaded seaweed, marine ferns, black periwinkles.

The boy looked for his favorite creatures, seahorses:
they'd ride the water column in single file
and look through the net's squares of wire mesh.
It was a protection zone, the other side,
beyond the pale. The mottled seahorses
could see into a cave where a groper lived,
and sensed somehow it couldn't get through the net.
Hovering there in clear sight of the old fish
they'd click and buck, as if they knew how to tease
the hungry, blue-eyed predator.

THE PHANTOM

My father was a fisherman who made
his own nets. He would use lengths
of horsehair for the crab snares.

On weekdays, he drove his horse
and cart to the Fisherman's Co-op;
Saturdays, he'd hitch up

a sulky and take me to Paddy's
Markets. It seemed he was always
working, except when

he drank at the Oaks Hotel.
He relaxed by reading paperback
Westerns, unless a new edition of

The Phantom had been released—
then he'd lay on the floor
and read it right through; we weren't

allowed to interrupt, if we did
it meant trouble. Our mother
would say, leave your father alone,

can't you see he's reading his Phantom.
The years went by and I wrote
many books, none of which he read.

Whenever we spoke, it was
about cars or fishing. He came
to see our new place on the Hawkesbury,

walked into my study—the walls
stacked with books and paintings—
looked about and considered

things, his eye fixed on a print,
a pop-art version of the Phantom,
then in a conspiratorial tone, he said,
'There he is.'

SUGARLOAF BAY,
MIDDLE HARBOUR

Marcia Hathaway, aged 32, was
fatally attacked by a bull shark, on
January 28th, 1963. She was wading
Sugarloaf Bay in Middle Harbour.

I fished here for leatherjackets
and the summer whiting—
in late winter a John Dory might drift
slowly through shallows
stalking angelfish. On the shore

lantana teemed with ticks;
kookaburras swooped for snakes,
sacred kingfishers aimed for whitebait.
On the slopes, fine houses
with swimming pools.

I'd overturn rocks on the shore
searching for pink nippers.
One day I watched a dollarbird tumble
down the sky and almost
hit the surface of the tide.

There were veils of barbecue smoke
smelling of sausages and onions
that drifted from the stern
of a Halvorsen cruiser at anchor;
children laughed and dogs barked in sunlight.

The green water was deep,
days were mostly blue—when it rained,
the orange domes of man-o'-war
jellyfish would break
the surface as they sailed along.

On windless mornings, the bay
stretched tight, a glass drum,
as if waiting for the vibration of an
unknown force, some dark fin that might cut
a pathway to civilization.

THE LONG BAY DEBATING SOCIETY

I spent my twenty-first in Long Bay Penitentiary
Each day in the front yards
We paced up and down
At night I read novels
And the poetry of Percy Shelley
Sometimes an education officer
Would turn up and ask
What are you going to do with your future?
I'd tell him I wanted to be a poet
He would shake his head
And comment I was being insolent
After weeks I convinced him
We wanted to start a debating team
There were plenty of crims
Who would join up
It took a month to convince the Governor
Finally the authorities agreed
We could form debating society
Things went well and we attended library
And researched our topics
Then came the day a team
From the outer agreed to come inside

And conduct a debate with us
However there was a condition
The Governor would choose the topic
Eventually the prison librarian
Ceremoniously handed us the Governor's note
(It was the summer of 1964) our topic
'Is the Sydney Opera House Really Necessary?'

THE CORIANDER FIELDS OF
LONG BAY PENITENTIARY

Serving two years hard;
my thoughts—sweet
as torn basil, or tinged
with broken roots
of coriander—soothe
fragmented fears.

When the mind's blank
I cultivate musky
persimmons, ideas
flutter, cabbage moths—
one with a lopsided wing
spins in circles.

I swallow, nothing's
left of my pride—
the prison doctor stitched
my cut wrists
without anesthetic,
his idea of punishment.

Laying with a blanket
on the bed-board,
I think of poppy fields
in the high country of Tasmania,
sun-splotched red blooms
loaded with seed,

their hairy stalks raked
by a wind from Antarctica;
here in my black slot,
an imaginary whiff
of opium mingles with
the bitter aftertaste of iodine.

INTERNAL WEATHER, FOR RANDOLPH STOW

I dwell in this bone-cave   rocking cup of skull
histories   constantly   rewriting themselves   weave

'brain waves' with drift   out from the body's net
a fatty backwash   veins of grainy information

blood cells   push into the white country
in multiples of ten   you know nothing's lost

we remembered   how sand   streamed in syllables
lines breaking into phrases   static sparks   weather breaks

rain-splattered paper   torn memories   the flicker
as sparks ping against blue tats   a pink tongue   so alive

touching porcelain   internal canals   the gush
woven nests   waves of fine hair   fragments of shells

cannot evaporate   can't die down   we live
at the world's expense   devouring   pale afterimages

with a bad weather eye   the serif-tails
chalk up   fine stainless blades   score the walls of arteries

a typewriter of bones   tapping   Morse on the spine's
fretwork   the philosopher   a machine   ticking out days

skidding down aisles in the supermalls   I stand here
in a column of breath   mixed with fine dust from red dirt

polishing fingernails   hair combed   dressed to
cast the same net   over leagues of broken weather

THE MIDNIGHT ZOO

for Sonya Hartnett

A bronze pigeon fans the humid air.
I follow its sleek calligraphy,
dancing, calling you back.
Under the colonial clock,
a Malvern Star, its front wheel
an echidna of broken spokes.
All night neon flickers
and says you know the way
as a snow leopard paws
the ground—forget the pigeon
becoming part of the bronze
distance. News from an unending
war breaks onto the airwaves,
it's Martha Gellhorn, correspondent,
attacking her typewriter.
We need space without time.
A pelican's beak-clack
by a lyrebird. The kids fall apart.
Parking meters tick away
in freshly enamelled metal jackets
on the verge of ignition.

The red glow and blue lights of the
city across the harbour—
or the Bridge pulsing green
and solemnly playing itself. Seagulls
breakfast on bogong moths
and black commas. Forget the warnings,
though don't leave your place,
this isn't official history anymore.

THE CONFESSIONS

after Saint Augustine

When my first love, Una,
was torn from my side
it crushed my heart.

We sent her back to Africa—
an obstacle to marriage
and advancement in Rome.

When she left, my diseased
soul fluttered above
my mother's glowing head.

Months passed. News
arrived—Una vowed she'd
never love another man.

Our son lived with me
inside the gates, grew up
without the sanction of wedlock.

Una lived alone
and drank wild honey
in attempts to ease the pain.

There'd be no healing.
Absence remained a wound,
although, a slave to lust, I took

a mistress; through long days
and streaky nights
my raw side festered.

Meanwhile, I was sinning
more and more—fully aware,
no matter what, there'd be no cure—

HARSH SONG

Afternoon's
pulse,
a feathery
susurration—
half song,
soft
leather
ratchet, or
breath
forced
through
a snake's
throat
across
the roof
of its
raked
mouth—
whispered
sounds,
a smoker's
thick
exhalation—
bowerbirds
in the grapevine.

SPINOZA

O my soul's friend
just once take

some advice
reach back

to myths of flight
measure

a peregrine falcon's
primary feathers

check semiplumes
for bird mites

then hold
your bearings

the law could
break by daylight

you can't afford
this luxury

after inventing
your new lucidity

tonight
open Ezekiel's gates

travel by light
shooting

through veins
and gelatinous

floating lenses
the packed neurons

composing
the optic nerves

of a peregrine's
four-dimensional sight

THE KINGFISHER'S SOUL

for Juno

A wave hits the shoreline of broken boulders,
Explodes, fans into fine spray, a fluid wing,
Then drops back onto the tide: a spume

Of arterial blood. Our eyes can be gulled by what
The brain takes in—our spirits take flight
Each time we catch sight out—feathers of smoke

Dissolve in air as we glide towards clarity.
In the old days I used to think art
That was purely imagined could fly higher

Than anything real. Now I feel a small fluttering
Bird in my own pulse, a connection to sky.
Back then a part of me was only half alive:

Your breath blew a thicket of smoke from my eyes
And brought that half to life. There's no
Evidence, nothing tangible, and no philosopher

Of blood considering possibilities,
Weighing up feathers, or souls. One day
Some evidence could spring from shadows

As my body did in rejecting the delicious poisons,
The lure of dark song. You came with a wind
In your gaze, flinging away trouble's screw,

Laughing at the King of Hell's weird command;
You created birthdays and the cheekbones
Of family—I was up, gliding through life

And my fabrications, thought's soft cradle.
I scoured memory's tricks from my own memory,
Its shots and scorecards, those ambiguous lyrics.

Clear birdsong was not human song, hearing became
Nets and shadowy vibrations, the purring
Air full of whispers and lies. I felt blank pages,

Indentations created by images, getting by
With the shapes I made from crafted habits.
You taught me how to weigh the harvest of light.

There was bright innocence in your spelling:
I learned to read again through wounded eyes.
Wispy spiders of withdrawal sparked with static

Electricity across skin, tiny veins, a tracery,
Live coppery wires, conducting pain to nerve
Patterns: all lightweights, to your blood's iron.

You brought along new light to live in
As well as read with—before you came, whenever
I caught a glimpse of my own blood, it seemed

A waterfall of bright cells as it bled away.
The clouds of euphony, created by its loss, became
Holes in thinking, pretend escape hatches.

A rush, wings through channels of my coronary
Arteries. We slept together when you conjured
A bed in your Paddington treehouse: barb-less hours,

Peace appeared and said: 'Soon, a future awaits you.'
I preferred the cover of night, yet here, I stepped
into the day by following your gaze.

ACKNOWLEDGMENTS

The poems in this selection first appeared in books as follows: *Canticles on the Skin* (Illumination Press, 1970): poems on pp. 3–8; *The Rumour* (Prism Books, 1971): poem on pp. 9–12; *Swamp Riddles* (Island Press, 1974): poems on pp. 13–28; *Cross the Border* (Hale & Iremonger, 1977): poems on pp. 29–39; *Where I Come From* (Big Smoke, 1979): poems on pp. 40–50; *The Law at Heart's Desire* (Prism Books, 1982): poems on pp. 51–63; *The Clean Dark* (Paper Bark, 1989): poems on pp. 67–93; *Wards of State* (HarperCollins, 1990): poem on p. 94; *Waving to Hart Crane* (Angus & Robertson, 1994): poems on pp. 95–107; *The Language of Oysters* (Craftsman Press, 1997): poems on pp. 108–11; *Black Water: Approaching Zukofsky* (Brandl & Schlesinger, 1999): poems on pp. 112–36; *Mulberry Leaves: New & Selected Poems 1970–2001* (Paper Bark, 2001): poems on pp. 137–49; *The Goldfinches of Baghdad* (Flood Editions, 2006): poems on pp. 153–78; *The Golden Bird: New and Selected Poems* (Black Inc., 2008): poems on pp. 179–87 and 223–25; *Net Needle* (Flood Editions, 2015): poems on pp. 188–222. Some of poems have been revised since their first publication, and in most cases, the most recent versions are included here.